For Danny, enjoy the book help many people

HYPNOTHER

METHODS, TECHNIQUES

&

PHILOSOPHIES

OF

FREDDY H. JACQUIN B.Sc

*Best Wishes
Freddy*

In the space between, illusion and perceived reality, resides the truth.

Jacquin · 2019

This is work is owned and published by Freddy Jacquin.
Hypnotherapy: Methods, Techniques and Philosophies of
Freddy H. Jacquin B.Sc.
Published 2018.

The right of Freddy H. Jacquin to be identified as the author of this work has been asserted by him in accordance with the UK Copyright, Designs and Patents Act 1988.

© Freddy H. Jacquin 2018 All rights reserved worldwide.

No part of this publication may be stored in a retrieval system, transmitted or reproduced in any way, including but not limited to digital copying and printing, without the prior agreement and written permission of the author.

You must not use this product for commercial use, except for the purposes of your own professional development, by which we mean that:

You may use this product as a reference for your own hypnosis sessions in accordance with acceptable practices, permissions and ethics; but

You may not claim to be associated with Freddy H. Jacquin in any way or use his name in connection with your own practice unless given permission by the author to do so.

Edited by Jesse Cummins.

Email: freddy.jacquin@gmail.com
Web: www.freddyjacquin.com

Cover designed by Felicia J Ursarescu

Acknowledgements

On my journey into the world of hypnosis and the discovery of my own self, through the ever expanding knowledge of the power and the weaknesses of the human mind, I have met some incredible people. Some have and continue to shape my thinking and actions.

Firstly I would like to thank my son Anthony for his on going support and inspiration. I am incredibly lucky to have him as a son, business partner and travelling companion.

Anthony is the author of the book 'Reality is plastic'. His book has inspired a complete generation of new Hypnotists across the globe. 'Reality is Plastic' is now believed by many to be the most comprehensive learning tool for those starting out in the field of hypnosis. RIP has also enabled Anthony and I to travel the world, teaching thousands of people these wonderful life changing skills.

Anthony, (I know that I am biased) is the most well read and knowledgeable person I know on the subject, and history of hypnosis, its origins and development, throughout the centuries.

I would like to thank my wife Marion for her continuous support.

Also my thanks to Jesse Cummins for his editorial skills.

Introduction:	1
The Big Question:	3
Magnetic Fingers:	8
Magnetic Fingers + emotion	
Jacquin Power Lift Induction:	11
Fractionation, Pattern Interrupt: Direct suggestion, Indirect suggestion, Ambiguous Touch:	
JPL Protocol:	13
Hand to Eye Induction:	14
Armotion Induction:	15
Progressive Induction (Body relaxation):	16
Pacing and Leading/Conscious, Unconscious. Induction:	18
<u>Therapeutic Techniques:</u>	
Therapeutic alliance:	21
Introduction to Parts Negotiation:	23
Parts Negotiation Therapy:	25
The Bridge, Parts Negotiation:	28
Parts Negotiation Therapy: + Post hypnotic suggestion:	29
Introduction to, The Arrow Technique:	35
Deborah's Story. The aggrieved wife.	
The Arrow Technique protocol:	41
The Jacquin Time Machine Technique:	43
The Jacquin Time Machine Technique, Protocol:,	46
Psychological/physiological Anchoring:	47
Anchoring: Protocol:	49
Power Anchor:	50
Self Hypnosis:	54
Anchoring a trance state:	55
Revivification induction:	56
Parts Negotiation + rewind visualisation to overcome phobias:	58
Jacquin Phobia Technique:	62
Metaphor/Indirect suggestion:	69
Physical healing /Quantum Healing:	81
The Power of the spoken word:	87
Jacquin Dream Architectural Therapy:	96
Psychological Decapitation:	97
Working with children:	100
Jacquin Total Perception Management (JTPM):	104
Smoking Cessation:	109
Quit Smoking Protocol:	119
Weight Loss:	122
Virtual gastric band:	129
Potensharu:	136
Covert Hypnosis Techniques:	186

HYPNOTHERAPY

Hypnosis for therapeutic healing and personal change.

The chances are that you have purchased this book either because you are an already practising hypnotherapist, you are interested in the subject of hypnosis, or you want to be able to help others change their lives for the better. This book has been written for just such a purpose, but it is not limited to only those that hypnotise or use hypnosis as a therapeutic tool.

My hope is that once you have read this book and understand how 'hypnosis' and 'trance' (I will often use those words to mean the same thing) can be used as a powerful agent for change, then you will share the knowledge with anyone who wants to help others.

My intention in writing this is so by the end of this book you will be able to hypnotise anyone who wants the experience, and also use the techniques in this book to help yourself and others.

Let me start by stating that everything that I will share with you in this book (stories, anecdotes, techniques and insights) have come from my own personal experience as a hypnotherapist.

Over the past 25 years I have worked with over 35,000 clients, and have seen amazing, sometimes seemingly miraculous changes take place within the client. Sometimes these changes occur within one session, and other times over a period of weeks or months.

The first thing for you to know and understand is that everything I have written within these pages is just my opinion, albeit an opinion based on real-life experience in the therapy room, but it is nevertheless just my opinion. All the cases that I speak of, either as a demonstration of a technique or to make a point, are real clients that I have personally seen. The evidence for the efficacy of the techniques in this book is only anecdotal, and you can choose to believe it or not.

Some of the cases and the outcomes will seem unbelievable, even miraculous, because they are.

I have heard it said that magic is magic to everyone except the magician, because he knows how the trick is done. I say that miraculous change brought about with the use of the techniques—hypnotic and otherwise—that you will learn in this book are miraculous even to the agent of change using them.

Although there continues to be research into the efficacy of hypnosis as a therapeutic tool, to date no definitive answer has yet been found. I will address this question later in this book.

I could fill this book by writing about the history of hypnosis, the main characters, some of their case studies and stories. I could fill it with quotes and cut and paste interesting facts from other books on hypnosis, as many writers do, and that would make this book thicker and seemingly more academic, but you can research and read about all of that online, if that is your thing.

In this book I am going to stick to just what I know through personal experience and insights that I have gleaned through actually doing this work.

I will speak as I would if you were standing here in front of me. I will attempt to teach you everything I know, to enable you, if it is your goal, to help others and in doing so help yourself.

Remember as you read this book that there is nothing I have learned, done or achieved with the use of hypnosis and the utilisation of the trance state that you cannot achieve for yourself.

The Big Question: What is Hypnosis?

I, of course, have my opinion as to what hypnosis is, as do a million other people, and the answer to that question will have almost as many answers. My mother had a counter question when asked a question that had no definitive answer, she would ask, 'how long is a piece of string?'

Before I get into what I think hypnosis is, let me first say that the same question can be asked of the mind. If you were to ask anyone if they have a mind, they would probably say yes. If you were to ask them where in the body the mind is, they would probably point to their head.

Medical scientists, neuroscientists, brain surgeons and the most eminent doctors using the most powerful MRI scanners have never seen or held a mind in their hands, yet if asked the question, 'do you have a mind?', they would say yes.

So here is the strange thing—the concept of 'the Mind' only exists in the mind, probably in the same place as the Spirit and the Soul, two other intangible parts of an organism known as a human being.

Therefore, if the mind only exists in our imagination, and imagination is created within the mind and hypnosis utilises the human ability to imagine, you may begin to see the problem academics have in describing—never mind proving—what hypnosis is. Or as my mother would say, 'how long is a piece of string?'

All the above having been said, I have personally helped people overcome heroin addiction, alcohol and drugs, anxiety, panic and chronic pain by using hypnosis and the techniques that you will learn from this book.

How is this possible using only your words and the imagination of the client? If you try and figure this out, you will be, as many academics studying this subject are, a very old and frustrated person. My suggestion (I am a hypnotist after all) would be that you learn these techniques and use them as soon as you can.

I was wondering about my lack of interest in the academic side of this fascinating subject, when a clear memory from my childhood came to me. I am one of five brothers (of which I am the oldest) and I have two sisters. When I was 11 years old my father bought the family's first car. All of us children were excited about days out to the seaside and other fun places. My father being a very analytical and curious man on the other hand wanted to know how the car worked. He spent the next few years taking the car apart and putting it back together again, in an attempt to find out how the combustion engine worked. While he did this, all we children wanted to do was go to the seaside.

I am sure that some of my clients have been fascinated by hypnosis when they have experienced seemingly miraculous changes in their life because of it. Some of them have even trained with me to become a hypnotherapist themselves. The majority of clients, though, don't care how hypnotherapy works. They just want the resolution to their problem, they just want to be happy again, or like me and my siblings, they just want to go to the seaside.

There are a lot of people in need of help. Let the academics spend their time studying the subject, while you go and use this wonderful and natural psychological tool.

In this book you will learn how to hypnotise almost anyone who wants to be hypnotised.

I hope that this book will bring you to the understanding that we are being hypnotised continuously, whether on purpose, accidentally by others, or from the constant chatter within our own heads.

So back to the big question: what is hypnosis? I believe that hypnosis is utilisation of an altered state of mind, and that any altered state of mind is an opportunity to give a suggestion that will stick, lodge, take hold and alter the way you think, feel and act.

Just for a moment think about an event in your past. Now if that is a clear memory, you will find that there is also a strong emotional element to that memory, and it is this emotional element that makes the memory clear.

When we think about altered states we tend to think of drug or alcohol induced altered states.

For me, any altered state can be utilised. If you are unhappy and I make you laugh or smile, I have altered your state. If you are happy and I make you sad, I have altered your state. If I make you angry, afraid, anxious or emotional, I have altered your state and whether intentionally or not I can give you a suggestion that can and probably will change the way you think.

Read this last paragraph over and over again until you get this, because this understanding will change your life and enable you to change the lives of others.

Imagine what you will achieve if every time someone altered your state—annoyed you, hurt you, made you laugh or any other emotional change—that you could give yourself a suggestion for what you want to achieve in your life, and then found yourself moving toward that goal, without thinking. When you see someone you love, whether it be a partner or child, who is emotional, laughing, crying, happy or sad, be ready with a positive suggestion that will help them achieve what they want in life. Without them realising that they had been given the suggestion they will find themselves achieving their goals.

You may already begin to see how easy it is to influence people without them knowing. By now you will have begun to realise that you don't have to be a hypnotist to do this. You are already doing it, whether you have realised it or not. Now you understand how to do this consciously, so your ability to influence people will increase beyond measure and you can use this knowledge to help others achieve what they want.

You can spend years and large amounts of money on hypnosis courses learning how to hypnotise someone. Don't look now, but on the next line in bold text, I will show you how. (You looked).

'Create an emotion and give a suggestion.' There it is. 'It can't be that easy?' I hear you say. 'It can't be that simple?' I hear you cry. Trust me it is. If I can (and I do know how to) create an emotional spike within you, I can influence you. I could suggest that you will not be able to see me, and you won't. I can suggest that you will feel no pain, and you won't.

I can suggest that you are fearless, and you will be, and I could suggest that you will feel happy and you will. This for me is what hypnosis is, and with this understanding comes the realisation that we are all being hypnotised continually.

We are continually being influenced, directed and manipulated without knowing that it is happening. We then assume wrongly that it is just our lack of discipline, personal strength, character or nature that makes us behave in ways that are detrimental or against what we really want to be or believe.

Do not despair though. I will show you how to hypnotise people slowly, rapidly, dramatically and progressively so that you have the option to choose how you want to hypnotise your subject.

When I first started work as a hypnotherapist, I believed, as the majority of hypnotherapists do, that people would come to see me with a problem. I would hypnotise them, put them into a trance, and then make them do what they wanted to do or stop them doing what they wanted to stop doing.

I would spend time relaxing the client while they sat in the chair with their eyes closed. I would worry about any outside noise in case they woke up. I now know that hypnosis has nothing to do with either relaxation or sleep—in fact hypnosis is the opposite to sleep. When hypnotised all of your senses are heightened. The hypnotised person can move, respond, speak, hear and feel whilst hypnotised, even with their eyes open.

You can and probably often are being hypnotised whilst walking down a busy street, drinking in a bar or club or watching TV. In these situations, you are not asleep, you do not have your eyes closed and may or may not be relaxed.

I now realise that my clients come to see me already in trance without knowing it, albeit negative and sometimes destructive trance states, but nonetheless hypnotised. My job is to take them out of the negative trance they are in and leave them in a positive trance.

As I stated earlier my intention is to teach you everything I know. This will include techniques for helping people overcome bad habits, addiction, fear, phobias, panic, depression, and eating disorders, including weight loss.

.

Firstly though, let us, as the song goes, 'start at the very beginning', with some powerful hypnotic inductions. Some of these inductions have been created and developed by me. These four inductions are: the Jacquin Power Lift induction, the Armotion induction, the Finger Lock induction and the Progressive induction. I will explain how and why these inductions work as we go through each technique.

Hypnotic induction: the vehicle that takes the subject or client from 'normal control' to hypnosis or trance.

It seems an obvious statement, but if there is an induction, there should also be an out-duction, although I have never heard it called that, in general it is referred to as the 'wake up'. This doesn't sit well with me because as you will come to learn, the hypnotised subject is not asleep, and if you are not asleep, how can you wake up?

So, I will call it the 'enduction' (end-duction). The simplest enduction is the count out. Which is as follows: "In a moment I will count to five. On 'four' your eyes will open and on 'five' everything will be back to normal." Then you count slowly to five.

Of course, the words in the enduction, 'everything will be back to normal' must be used if you are doing stage hypnosis and have been suggesting that the hypnotised person experience silly or strange things. On the other hand, if you are doing therapeutic work and your suggestions to your clients are for positive emotions, physical healing, or positive behavioural changes, then you want to leave the client in a positive trance. I will explain how to do this later on, when we discuss therapeutic techniques.

I will teach you later on in this book how to hypnotise people without them knowing (covert hypnosis). To begin with though, let us start with some of my favourite overt hypnosis inductions.

This first induction utilises the client's imagination and ability to experience a rapid, emotional change in order to trip them into trance. I use this induction in almost every hypnotic, first encounter, and have personally used it with over 30,000 clients, and with hundreds of thousands of people online. Do not under estimate the power of this simple technique.

Magnetic Fingers

Look at this induction/technique as your first baby steps on the road to hypnotic power. You will see as you practice this technique that it contains all of the elements that you will learn to use in hypnosis: imagination, suggestion, altered state, indirect and direct commands, and in the second example, emotion.

This technique enables you to practice hypnotising so as to gain confidence and belief in yourself as a hypnotist. It will enable you to utilise your language, the pace, control and tone.

As with all the techniques, I will explain how to do it, and then break down the elements, to describe why it works.

Firstly, do this yourself, follow my instructions to the letter:

(1) Clasp your hands tightly together.

(2) Bend your elbows so that your hands are level with your face.

(3) Keeping your hands clasped together, pull your index fingers an inch apart, pointing up toward the ceiling.

(4) Focus on the gap between your fingers and imagine that they are magnetised and pulling together.

(5) Watch as they move automatically together and touch, close your eyes for a second and then open them.

(6) Separate your hands.

If you followed these instruction, you will have experienced your fingers pulling together like magnets.

This could be dismissed as a playground trick, as there is a physiological reason for this to happen. However, you are going to turn this natural experience into a hypnotic induction.

Firstly, an explanation of the difference between compliance (an instruction that is carried out willingly) and a hypnotic suggestion (a suggestion that something physical will happen, that then occurs without any conscious control). This could be described as the difference between something you are doing and something that is felt as just happening automatically. Hypnotic language and suggestion turns a doing into a happening.

How do we as hypnotists achieve this? We are going to create an emotion, a change of emotional state, and then give a hypnotic suggestion.

I would like you to do the same exercise as before, but with a subtle twist.

Magnetic fingers with emotion:

(1) Clasp your hands tightly together.

(2) Bend your elbows so that your hands are level with your face.

(3) Keeping your hands clasped together, pull your index fingers an inch apart, pointing up toward the ceiling.

(4) Focus on the gap between your fingers and imagine that they are magnetised and pulling together.

(5) Watch as they move automatically together and touch, close your eyes for a second.

(6) Think about the person or people you love most, see their face, feel that love.

(7) As you feel that love, imagine that your hands are stuck tightly together and that there is nothing you can do to get them unstuck. When you realise they are stuck, try to pull them apart and find that you cannot.

(8) This will last for five seconds and then your hands will come apart.

If you experienced the feeling that your hands were actually stuck together for a few moments, then you have just experienced hypnotic phenomena.

Read and memorise the steps,, and then find someone who wants to experience hypnosis. Deliver the instruction with total confidence, as there is no doubt that the person's hands will be stuck together.

The only difference between the two above exercises is the introduction of emotion. Practice this exercise as often as you can with as many people as you can.

When you step up to hypnotise someone, BE THE HYPNOTIST. Act as if you have no doubt that they will be hypnotised and deliver your words with total confidence. Be prepared to fail a few times, but expect to be successful and you will be amazed how often you are.

The Jacquin Power Lift Induction

As with the other inductions, this induction can be used almost anywhere. I generally use this induction within the therapeutic setting. I created this induction utilising fractionation, pattern interruption, direct and indirect suggestion and an ambiguous touch technique. Although in general our clients will be sitting down, this induction can be carried out with someone who is standing up. I will describe the technique as if the client is sitting down.

I will explain what the terms, 'fractionation', 'pattern interrupt', 'direct and indirect suggestions' and 'ambiguous touch', mean.

Fractionation

You start to take someone into hypnosis and then bring them back up. You do this a few times, each time suggesting that they will experience going deeper into hypnosis.

Pattern Interrupt

As human beings we are very easily trained. If we do something often enough, we create an unconscious pattern of behaviour that enables us to learn rapidly and function at a high level. Reading is an obvious example—it would be impossible for you to 'not' to read this.

If we interrupt an unconscious pattern, for example if I were to place a Russian word in the middle of this sentence, then for a moment your brain would be confused. That moment of confusion can be utilised by a hypnotist to give a very direct suggestion that will very likely be acted upon without question.

This is my favourite verbal confusion pattern-interrupt technique:
You take your client's hand and start to swing it gently from side to side, whilst looking them directly in their eyes.
You ask them, 'Are you in a trance, not in a trance?'
Then without waiting for an answer you ask them, 'What is it that you are not thinking about, that you don't know you know?'
As you say this you will notice that their eyes will glaze over for a split second whilst they try and make sense of the question. In that moment you give their hand a gentle tug and say, 'Sleep'.

Direct suggestion

Examples of direct suggestions: 'You may feel yourself going deeper into hypnosis.', 'The need for a cigarette will be gone.', 'You will no longer be afraid.'

Indirect suggestion

An example of an indirect suggestion: 'I had a client who sat in that chair. She relaxed and drifted into a deep hypnotic trance.'

Ambiguous Touch

This technique to create catalepsy, although easy enough to learn, may require some practice.

Take the client's wrist with your thumb on the inside of the wrist, your middle finger on the outside of the wrist and your index finger on the back of the wrist.

Direct the client to look directly into your eyes.

You focus your gaze at the space between their eyes.

You lift their arm with the ambiguous-touch grip described above.

You then slowly remove your thumb and middle finger from the wrist leaving the index finger touching the back of their wrist. Now if the client's arm remains in position, you remove your index finger from their wrist, leaving their arm now floating in mid-air. You then point this out to the client at the same time as suggesting that they cannot get their arm down. When the client tries and fails, you have created arm catalepsy.

Jacquin Power Lift Induction - Protocol

Having asked the client whether they are ready to be hypnotised, and having gotten an agreement that they are, explain what you are going to do.

Say, "I will show you what I am going to do and then I will do it."

Point at one of their hands and say, "In a moment I will pick up that hand."

Demonstrating on yourself, say, "As I pick your hand up to here", take your left wrist with your right hand and bend your elbow, lift it up and say, "You can allow your eyes to close."

Demonstrate this and the following on yourself.

Then say, "Then as I push your hand down your eyes will open. As I pull your hand up your eyes will close and as I push your hand down your eyes will open. That is all I am going to do. Is that alright?"

Get agreement from the client. Then as you're reaching toward their hand, ask if you "can borrow that arm". This is a strange thing to say, but it implies that for a while that arm is yours to use.

Taking the client's wrist in your hand, lift it slowly, using ambiguous touch and saying, "Allow your eyes to close."

Hesitate for a few seconds and then while pushing it down slowly, say, "And as I push it down you can allow your eyes to open as you relax even more."

Repeat this, but this time as you pull their hand up say, "As I lift your hand up, your eyes will close, and as I push your hand down, open your eyes and relax even more."

Repeat this, but this time as soon as their hand reaches the up-position you change your tone of voice, squeeze their wrist lightly and say with authority, "Feel your wrist stiffening."

With your free hand, poke their forearm muscle and say, "Feel your forearm muscle stiffening."

Letting go of their wrist, but keeping your finger lightly on the arm, poke their elbow and say, "Feel your elbow locking."

Take your finger from the forearm, poke the client gently in the shoulder and say, "Shoulder locking, muscles tightening. Arm going completely rigid now."

> Run your finger under their wrist as you say, "And as that hand just hangs there now, you can go deeply into hypnosis

Hand-to-Eye Induction

Once again, this induction can be carried out and used in any situation or environment. You will become aware now that you have learned the previous induction that taking someone into hypnosis is simple, but relies upon the attitude and expectation of the hypnotist. That applies to this induction as well.

1) Ask the question "Are you ready to be hypnotised?". Having gotten agreement, point at one of their hands and ask the question "Can I borrow that arm?". Without waiting for the answer, reach over and lift their hand toward their face, palm facing inward.

2) Point at the palm of their hand with your free hand and direct their visual attention to it by saying "focus on one line, one spot on your hand."

3) As you give this instruction, gently push their hand toward their face, saying, "Notice the changing focus of your eyes as your hand moves toward your face. As you notice your eyes, close your eyes." As they close their eyes you push their hand gently but firmly onto their face and with command in your voice say "Sleep".

4) As you do this you push their head gently forward with your other hand. You can now deepen the trance with the suggestions for going deeper, relaxing more and more, and so on. If the client is standing, then you should tell them that their legs will continue to support them as they go deeply into hypnosis.

This induction from start to finish generally takes no more than three minutes to complete. You will find that once you start using hypnosis as a therapeutic tool for change the limits of what you can help people achieve depends solely on the client and your own limiting beliefs—or should I say lack of them.

Armotion - Induction

This is an eye-open induction. The hypnotised person will experience hypnosis without "relax", "sleep" or "deeper and deeper" being used, which many hypnotists seemed to deem necessary to induce trance.

I usually use this induction in an impromptu situation, although it can be used at any time.

As with the other inductions that you will learn, creating emotion is the key and your confidence is imperative. Assuming that the subject has agreed to be hypnotised:

1) Point at their right hand and say "Can I borrow that arm?". Without waiting for confirmation,

2) Reach over and while holding the person's wrist, lift their arm up to shoulder height, making sure that their arm is straight. While you do this,

3) Direct them to look directly into your eyes. Using 'the hypnotic gaze' (focus your eyes on an imagined spot behind the subject's eyes),

4) Ask the subject to think about the person or people whom they love most. This is done in the same way and with the same words that you learned in the Magnetic Fingers induction. As soon as you perceive an emotional shift in the subject's emotional state,

5) Gently let go of their wrist, leaving the arm in mid-air. You must keep their focus on your eyes as you do this.

6) Point out that their arm is still in the position even though you are no longer holding it. As they look toward their arm,

7) Say: 'Imagine that your arm is suspended all by itself and there is nothing you can do about it and when you realise that there is nothing you can do about it, TRY and push it down and find that you cannot'.

The moment that they try and fail to push their arm down they are in trance and how you proceed from there is entirely up to you.

Progressive induction

A progressive induction is an induction that takes the client/subject into a trance in a slow, progressive way. This can take anything between 5 and 15 minutes.

This can be a body relaxation technique in which the hypnotist suggests muscle relaxation, or a verbal pacing-and-leading technique. I will describe both. You can use the words as a script, but remember not to treat the words as if they are a spell. Read the words with meaning and intent. It may help to pace your words with the inhalation and exhalation of your client's breathing. This will, if you do it correctly, create an unconscious rapport with your clients. Remember: Practice makes perfect.

Body Relaxation Induction

With a body relaxation induction, I would suggest that as you do this you allow yourself the time with each suggestion to experience the relaxation in your own muscles. This will enable your client to have the time to do the same.

Body Relaxation Induction - Protocol - Script

If you are ready to be hypnotised, take a breath in, and as you breath out, allow your eyes to close.

With your eyes now closed you can begin to relax.

I want you for a while to focus on your body.

Start with the top of your head and allow your scalp to relax.

Imagine that you are having your scalp massaged and that all the tension is leaving your scalp.

Let that feeling of relaxation spread down to your eyes.

Imagine the little muscles around your eyes relaxing.

Imagine that they are relaxing so completely they just won't work.

Imagine that every word I say is relaxing them so completely that they just won't work.

Imagine that those muscles are relaxing automatically.

When you realise that your eyes are so relaxed they just won't work, you can test them and find that they are completely locked and that there is nothing you can do about that now. That's right.

Let that relaxation spread down to your jaw and allow those muscles in your jaw to relax completely now.

Allow your tongue to relax in your mouth.

The muscles in your neck relax completely.

Let that feeling spread down to your shoulders.

Imagine you are having your shoulders massaged, feel those muscles relaxing completely.

Let that feeling spread to your arms, your biceps, your forearms, your wrists, hands and fingers.

As you do that you may become aware of certain sensations.

For a moment focus on your breathing.

Imagine that you are breathing in calm and breathing out tension.

Breathing in calm and breathing out tension.

Allow the muscles in your chest to relax.

Let that feeling to spread down to your stomach.

Your hips, your thighs and your legs.

Allow that feeling to spread to the muscles in your calves, ankles, feet and toes.

Let every muscle relax completely, just like a handful of rubber bands thrown on the chair, loose and relaxed.

Now every word I say is going to relax you even more.

And the more relaxed you become the deeper you will go.

Conscious/Unconscious, dissociation.
Progressive, Pacing and Leading induction.

The theory that underpins this induction is that we have a conscious and unconscious mind and this induction aims to distract the conscious mind and leave the unconscious mind available and open to suggestion. This is done by statements of fact about things that you know the client is consciously experiencing, and statements of fact that the client is not consciously aware of until you draw their attention to it. Here is an example: 'You are reading these words.' This is something you are consciously aware of). 'You can become aware of your heart beating.' This is something you are unaware of until brought forth. The hypnotist will lead the client into hypnosis by making statements that will lead the client into an inner focus of attention.

The Script:

If you are ready to be hypnotised, take a breath in, and as you breathe out, allow your eyes to close.

With your eyes now closed you can begin to relax.

Although at times you may be more aware of some things than you were before.

The sound of my voice.

The comfort of the chair.

The sounds in the room.

Sensations in arms and legs.

The sounds outside the room.

The sound of your breathing.

The beating of your heart.

And the thoughts and images that enter the mind automatically.

Just for a moment think about the people you love.

See their faces and feel that love.

Let that feeling of love remind you of your real worth, your real value.

As a person, as a being.

Because with the eyes closed it becomes easier.

To become more aware of a variety of things that otherwise may go overlooked or ignored.

Thoughts, feelings, sensations and the love that you may have overlooked before.

Because with the eyes closed it becomes easier for the conscious mind to continue that letting go.

Letting go of the effort it takes to be aware of exactly where the arms are positioned or the hands or fingers. Even the effort it takes to be aware of which leg seems to relax more quickly or completely than the other may seem to be too much effort to bother making. It's so much easier simply to relax and feel yourself drifting down.

Down toward a place of quietness.

A place of peaceful inner awareness.

Where even the effort it takes to be aware of the sound of my voice or the meaning of my words may almost seem to be too much effort to bother making.

It is so much easier, simply to relax and let go.

In your own time and in your own way.

Drifting down, deeper and deeper down, now.

Ten, twenty, a hundred times deeper, now.

Every word I say now will take you deeper.

And as you drift even deeper, my voice, my words will drift with you to become a part of your experience now.

And the deeper you go the better you will feel, and the better you feel the deeper you will go.

Now, nothing bothers you, nothing affects you and nothing disturbs you.

All that matters now is the sound of my voice and achieving your goal.

Everything I say now becomes your reality and every suggestion I give you, you will act upon without hesitation, becomes your reality.

You have a conscious mind and an unconscious mind, and that unconscious mind, the back of the mind, can continue to hear, and respond to those things I may say, without the need for you to do anything at all.

Letting go even of the effort it may take, to tell the exact position of arms, legs and the entire body now that seems to drift through time and space.

The unconscious mind drifts without boundaries, without borders.

See yourself at a time in the future having achieved your goal and look back to now and notice all the things that you did, and changed, that led to achieving that goal.

The unconscious mind can make those changes now.

As the conscious mind drifts off some place else entirely, now.

That's right, in your own time and in your own way.

A drifting down, deeper, deeper, deeper down.

And as you drift even deeper, I can wonder whether you are aware that you have drifted deeply into hypnosis.

Because the deeper you go the better you will feel and the better you feel the deeper you will go.

Ten, twenty a hundred times deeper now.

Every word I say now will take you deeper.

And as you drift even deeper my voice, my words will drift with you to become a part of your experience now.

And as you drift even deeper you can use your unconscious mind as a resource that you can learn from and really have an experience.

Now that you know how to induce hypnosis, you may like to know how you can help others achieve freedom from limiting beliefs, irrational fears, and destructive habits and behaviours.

The following techniques in this book will enable you to do so.

<u>Therapeutic Alliance</u>

Let me first state that when it comes to lasting behavioural or physical change, one thing is of paramount importance. Although it may be assumed that when a client or friend asks for your help in overcoming a problem that they want to change, it is not always necessarily the case. I will, and I ask you to also to always ask the question, 'Do you want to change?'.

Often clients will ask me to help them quit smoking, drugs or drinking too much alcohol, because their wife, husband or doctor says they should. That is not a good enough reason and I will not work with someone if the desire to change their life, is not theirs. It doesn't matter how much you want to change for someone else, the change will not last, unless you want it.

Examples of where the desire to change is not the client's true desire.

A client came to see me seeking my help to enable her to lose a stone/7kg/14lb in weight. When I asked her for her reasons for wanting to lose the weight (because in my opinion she was a perfectly healthy weight and a lovely woman) she said, 'My husband is into designer clothes, watches and cars, and he thinks I would look better if I lost weight.'. I asked the client if she thought she would look or feel better if she lost weight and she told me that she thought she looked fine as she was, but her husband, whom she wanted to please, thought differently.

I told the client that I could help her, 'but', I said, 'in reality, the wrong person was sitting in the therapy chair'. I told her, rightly or wrongly, that unfortunately, she would never be thin enough, tall enough or blonde enough, to satisfy her husband's need to impress others.

During the hypnotherapy session, as I do with all my clients, I endeavoured to give the lady an understanding of her true worth and value as a woman, mother and person, so that she could make her own decisions about her life.

A statement that I often make to weight-loss clients when we meet for the first time is this: there are some things we cannot change, but how much we weigh is not one of them. There is only one real question when it comes to weight loss, and that is, 'How badly do I want to look or feel that good?'. The great motivator and personal-change guru Anthony Robbins says, 'If you can find a big enough "WHY TO" you can always find the "HOW TO".'

My son Anthony had a client who had come to see him to quit smoking. Anthony asked the man why he was there. The man said that he had three heart operations, he had breathing problems, his circulation was poor, and the doctor had told him that he wanted him stop smoking, because if he didn't quit, he would die. So, Anthony said that he understood how ill the cigarettes had made him and then asked the client, 'but do you want to quit smoking?' The man laughed and said emphatically, 'NO, I don't want to quit, I love my cigarettes, I am only here to please my wife'. Anthony politely explained that the man should go away and have a serious think about what was really important in his life, and that when he decided that he really wanted quit smoking, for his own reasons, to book another appointment.

I had a client who had had a cancerous kidney removed. He had been told by his surgeon that if he quit smoking he had as much chance of living to old age as anyone else, but if he continued to smoke he may only have a few more years. The client had two young daughters. The first thing the client said to me when he walked into my office was, 'this is going to be a challenge'. I told him that if it was going to be a challenge that I would lose. I explained that I am not a therapist to challenge people, but if he wanted my help and truly wanted to quit smoking, I would do my utmost to help him. We went ahead with the session. In those days I used to give a money-back guarantee with my quit-smoking clients. The next day the man (as I expected), phoned my office and asked for his money back. I remember thinking at the time that because he was determined to challenge me instead of working with me, I had lost an hour of my time, but he may have lost twenty years of his life.

Introduction to Parts Negotiation

I mentioned earlier that I use what I call a parts negotiation. Let me explain what this is and how and why I use it.

As human beings we have the ability to learn things—sometimes incredibly complex things: reading writing, languages, the use of complex machinery, cars, bicycles, and musical instruments, to name but a few. Thousands of wonderful skills, and we learn them so well that we can do these things without even thinking. You have been doing your laces up for years, but I doubt you could tell me which hand goes over which first and yet you have carried out that task thousands of times.

This ability to learn something and then allow it to become something that happens automatically enables us to function at the level that we function at. If we had to think about walking—I'm going to put this foot here and this foot here, balance, take another step, balance—if we had to think about walking, our mind would be so full of walking we would not be able to focus on anything else.

Now as I said this ability enables us to do so many things and function so well in this wonderful world of the 21st century. Where it works against us is when we learn a habit such as smoking, nail biting, cocaine sniffing or anything else that may end up killing us. For the smoker to stop smoking, the weight-loss client to stop snacking, or the drug addict to stop killing themselves would be as difficult as you trying to forget how to walk or speak. You may be able to really focus and do it for a while but the moment you are distracted from focusing on the thing you are trying not to do, you will go back to doing it again.

So, what the hell has this got to do with 'parts' I hear you ask? Well, be patient and I will continue to explain.

When we learn something to the point where it becomes an automatic function, ability or skill that we can do without thinking, it's as if we create a part of us that then runs that process. Let us take the smoking habit as an example. I see clients that have smoked 30 cigarettes a day for 30+ years and I say to them that that is an incredible feat. To remember to do something thirty times a day, every day for thirty years without fail is extraordinary. You could not possibly do that consciously. At some point in a smoker's life they decide that it is important that they remember to smoke a cigarette and then learn to do it to the point where it becomes an automatic function, and at that point they create a part of them that then does that job for them so that they can focus on other things.

If you are a driver, you have a part of you that can drive whilst you are talking to your passenger or eating or thinking about where you have been on holiday. The part that knows how to drive is monitoring the road, making thousands of adjustments on the steering wheel, working the brake, the accelerator and indicating whilst you are thinking of something else entirely.

Yes, you have a part of you that can drive, a part of you that can read—try and not read the next word and find that you can't not read it—it is impossible. We develop and create these parts of us to do these jobs so that we can focus on more interesting things.

We even speak in these terms: 'I would love to lose weight, but there is a part of me that just loves cake. I would love to get up and dance, but there is a part of me that will not let me. I would love to quit smoking, but there is a part of me that keeps lighting the cigarettes up even though it's killing me.' We use these terms to describe some of the actions we take.

Very few of these parts are negative or destructive. The majority are useful and protective, and all of these parts start life as a positive intention. This may be hard to accept—how can pulling your eyelashes out or cutting yourself be in any way positive? However, I would ask you to start with the belief that behind EVERY behaviour, good or bad, there is a positive intention. So, the idea behind 'Parts Negotiation Therapy' is that with the use of hypnosis we can communicate with the part that runs the process, whatever that may be, and get it to do something else, something more beneficial for the client.

Part Negotiation Therapy

Elicit what it is that the client wants to achieve. To be a non-smoker, to be free of the fear, to lose weight, etc. Explain in your own words (or mine if you prefer) how we create a part of us that runs the negative behaviour or habit they want to change. Explain that you will set up an unconscious line of communication with that part and that it will communicate in some way.

Maybe it communicates through an unconscious automatic movement of some kind. You will ask that part to explain what has been trying to do for them (the positive intention behind the habit or behaviour). You will ask the part to go to their creative mind, the part of them that dreams, makes plans, has ideas and solutions, and allow that creative mind to come up with some other way of satisfying the positive intention that has nothing to do with the old way.

Something else that it can do that is of benefit that is at least as immediate and effective, but which will allow the client to have the life and the health and happiness that they desire. Tell the client that you will then ask the part to choose one of the new choices and integrate that new behaviour or habit into their life. Explain that when that happens their life will change, and the detrimental behaviour or habit will be gone, replaced by something positive and beneficial to their life.

Parts Negotiation Therapy

I will use parts negotiation therapy with my clients in every first hypnotherapy session.

Below, I will use a habit problem as a demonstration.

The joy of the parts negotiation protocol is that you (the therapist) do not have to know what the fear or problem is in order to help. How can this be? Surely you need to know the problem so that you can decide on a strategy and the correct protocol to use? Well, no, you don't. Obviously, you will ask the client or friend how you can help them, or what it is they want to change, and in general they are going to tell you. With parts negotiation therapy though it is not necessary to know.

This is how I proceed.

The client presents with a habitual problem. I will listen as they tell me the problem. Now the majority of people start by saying the things they don't want to feel or be anymore. Some will want to tell you their theory on why they behave the way they do. This may be interesting, but to me it is of no consequence.

As soon as I can, without being rude, I will ask the question, 'What do you want? How do you want to feel or be?' Sometimes the client will look at you with a blank expression on their face, because they have spent their lives focused on what they don't want.

If this occurs I will sometimes ask what I call the Magic Wand question, which goes like this. 'If I could wave a magic wand and you were free of this problem, how would you be?'

Let's take the most common habit that clients present with: smoking cigarettes. When the client says, 'I will be free of the smoking habit, I will be healthier, have more money and be happier.' I will sit back as if it has just occurred to me, and say, 'So you don't want to smoke anymore? It's killing you and costing you, but it's as if there is a part of you that continues to light the cigarette even though you don't want to do it anymore?'

Not one of the 30,000+ clients I have seen has said 'no that's not what it's like'. I have asked the question in rooms with two hundred clients in a group session and two hundred heads have nodded in agreement. Whether it is one client or two hundred I continue with these words, 'Well in a moment I am going to hypnotise you and I will speak directly to the part of you that is running the smoking habit and it will communicate. I will ask it what it is trying to accomplish for you. I will then ask it to go to your creative mind and find something else to do for you that is at least, if not more immediate, effective and beneficial for you that has nothing to do with smoking. When that happens the need for a cigarette will be gone.

As you can imagine at this point the client may think that they have walked into a parallel universe. Two minutes earlier you appeared to be quite normal and now you are suggesting that you are going to be communicating with some invisible part of them. Worry not, if you do this correctly—and you will if you follow my directions to the letter—the client will have an undeniable experience of hypnotic phenomena and unconscious communication.

This next paragraph is what I call the bridge: the transition from the induction to unconscious communication with the client's unconscious mind.

You may want to learn this verbatim and memorise it, because at this point you will be focused on looking for the ideo-motor signals (unconscious movements) when they occur.

Parts Negotiation:
The Bridge between the induction and the actual parts negotiation;

Script

Now as you go even deeper into hypnosis you can use your unconscious mind as a resource that you can learn from and really have an experience, one that is satisfactory to you.

All that is needed to build a good rapport with the unconscious is to have a line of communication. Sometimes the unconscious communicates with movement. It may be that the eyes flicker or the head nods slightly to indicate 'yes'. Or a muscle twitches involuntarily to indicate 'no'. It may be that your left hand starts to lift and drifts up to indicate 'yes', or your right hand, lifts even higher. Only the unconscious mind knows which it will use, because the unconscious mind knows more about you than anyone else. So, as you drift even deeper I would like your unconscious mind to search and find one thing, one thing that is of vital and utmost importance to your life, health and happiness and when it has found it I would like that signal to occur with honest unconscious movements.

"This may be a good time to give you my theory on what I believe your unconscious mind is created to do for you. Remember this is just my opinion, but this belief makes it easier for me to do Parts Negotiation Therapy, so that is why I am explaining it now. I believe that behind every behaviour your unconscious mind is only ever trying to achieve one of two things for you. It is either trying to protect you or it is trying to give you pleasure. All you have to do when working with a 'Part' of a client or a friend, is to decide which of these two things the behaviour the person is presenting with is trying to achieve. Once you have decided, then it is easy to name the part."

If it is a habitual problem, thumb sucking, nail biting, smoking, eating, etc. then you may say, 'I would like to speak to the part that runs the smoking habit, that runs the nail biting habit, etc.'

If it's a fear, phobia, panic attacks, anxiety, stress, blushing, confidence, etc. You may say, 'I would like to speak to the part that runs the protective mechanism.' You can use this name for any behaviour that you deem to be protective.

Healing: the part that runs the immune system.

Weight-loss: the part responsible for eating, exercising and the metabolism.

Performance: The part responsible for their ability to achieve.

As you can see when it comes to naming the 'part' it is only limited by your imagination or as my mum would say, 'how long is a piece of string'.

So here is how you actually use the parts negotiation in the therapy session.

(1) Hypnotise the client with your preferred induction.

(2) Ask the client's unconscious mind to search for something that they want to change or feel differently about.

(3) Set up an unconscious communication (signal).

(4) Ask the unconscious mind to hand the signal to the part responsible for the behaviour that the client wants to change. Get a signal that this has happened.

(5) Ask that part to explain to the client at some level of consciousness what it is that it is trying to achieve for them. What the positive intention behind the behaviour is. Ask that part to allow you to know when the client has that understanding by allowing the signal to occur. Get a signal.

(6) Ask the part to go to the client's creative mind and find lots of new choices, other ways of achieving for them the positive intention of the behaviour that will at the same time allow them freedom from the negative effects of that behaviour. Get at least three signals.

(7) Ask the part to choose one of the new choices, the one that it believes is the most effective. Get a signal.

(8) Ask the part to integrate the new choice into the client's mind and body, and to let you know when it has done so by allowing the signal to occur. Get a signal.

(9) Thank the part for communicating and for making the changes.

Below is a true case of mine of one of the stranger examples of a parts negotiations that I have experienced.

Case: The Man with the Phobic Foot

The client asked for my help in what was a very unusual problem. He could not drive his car over any bridge. He was not afraid of bridges, heights or driving and he really wanted to travel.

The gentleman was in his sixties when he came to see me and had been driving without a problem for over forty years. Then one day whilst driving toward a bridge which he wanted to pass over, his right foot refused to press the accelerator pedal down.

He initially thought he may have a cramp, although he had no pain, so he pulled over and stopped the car. As soon as he had turned off the engine his foot returned to normal. Thinking that the cramp had gone, he set off again only to find that as he approached the bridge again the same thing happened—he could not accelerate.

In desperation and with no small amount of frustration he turned the car around and set off the way he came, and his foot worked perfectly normally. As anyone would, he turned the car around again and headed back to the bridge only to find that the exact same thing happened again and no matter how hard he tried he could not push the accelerator down when he got to the bridge.

As he and his wife were travelling to Wales on holiday, his wife took over the driving duties and they had their holiday. This the man told me had occurred two years previously and in the past two years he had all kinds of physiotherapy and other therapy including CBT and counselling and still the problem persisted. As a last resort, and much to the man's disgust, he was talked into seeing a Hypnotherapist. As with a lot of people, especially men of a certain age, hypnotherapy was in the man's words, 'a load of mumbo jumbo'.

So, having listened to the man's story and the list of therapies he had already tried, I said to the man and his wife (who had come to give him moral support), 'So, you have tried to overcome this and have had lots of therapists talking to you, and you want to be able to drive over bridges, but your right foot refuses to press the pedal down, correct?' The man said, 'yes', turning to his wife who was nodding in agreement. 'Well' I said, 'then there is no point in talking to you, I will speak directly to your right foot and ask it what it is up to, and it will communicate.' If the man had doubted my sanity when he first met me, now he had no doubts.

Ignoring the look of disbelief on the man's face I asked him to focus his eyes on his right foot, which for some unknown reason even to him, he did.

I then proceeded to ask his foot whether it would be willing to communicate with me.

To the astonishment of the man and his wife, his foot twitched violently. The man realised that he was not making his foot move—it was happening by itself. As the man stared at his foot, I ask his foot to explain to the man at some level of consciousness what it was trying to do for him. The man's foot twitched again. I said then go ahead and when he understands the reason at whatever level that it could let me know. After 30 seconds with the man still staring at his foot, it twitched again.

I then asked his foot to find other ways of protecting him and keeping him safe but at the same time allowing him to drive over bridges again. I reassured his foot that it didn't have to take any of the new choices, but to let me know when it had found one that it believed would keep him safe, one that would allow him to travel freely once again. After a while the man's foot twitched again.

I then asked the man's foot to take this new choice and integrate it into his life so that he could be happy and drive freely again and to let me know when this was done. A few seconds later his foot twitched again. I then thanked the foot for communicating and making the changes for the man.

The client slowly looked up at me as if he had seen a ghost. His wife was still sitting opened-mouthed. I asked the man to close his eyes which he did without question. I then said, 'In a moment I will count to five. On "four" your eyes will open and on "five" you will feel incredible and this will never affect you again.' I then gave him some double bind suggestions (I will explain those later), took his payment and said goodbye.

The man called me later to tell me that on leaving my office he had driven to the closest bridge and driven over it without any problem from his foot. He said that he still doesn't know what had happened in my office, and he didn't think he had been hypnotised, but said he really didn't care. He thanked me and said goodbye. Over the years he has referred many clients to me.

Parts Negotiation + post hypnotic suggestion

Case: The Couple Who Tried Too Hard

The pleasure and satisfaction that I get from this 'job' cannot be described in words, but sometimes people touch you with their story and this case is one that I will remember forever.

Unlike the movies in which all the therapy clients tend to be beautiful and rich, in real life, at least in mine, most of the clients that I see are ordinary people doing ordinary jobs, and like the majority of us, just trying to get through the best they can.

A young couple came to see me because they had been trying to get pregnant to no avail and they had heard from a friend that I had helped her conceive.

As with most couples in the same situation, they were reading books, taking temperatures, watching the clock and at what was supposed to be exactly the right moment, having sexual intercourse.

They had all the tests done by their doctor, who had told them that there was no apparent reason why the wife shouldn't conceive. Having tried to get pregnant for the past two years they had decided to have IVF treatment, but as a last resort before the expense and disruption of IVF treatment, decided to see the strange, bald, 'foot-talking-to' hypnotist.

One of my hypnotist heroes is Dr Milton Erickson, who was an MD, psychiatrist and probably the most influential hypnotherapist of all time. A book by Jay Hayley about Erickson's work called 'Uncommon Therapy' details some of his case studies.

In the book he tells of a couple of uptight college professors who were trying to have a baby together. They had been married for some years and like the couple in my story they were trying to get pregnant. I won't go into the Erickson story here, but if you like reading about genius, buy the book Uncommon Therapy.

Back to my experience. The young couple in my therapy room were, as most people are when first in the company a hypnotist, slightly anxious, and not without trepidation at what I was going to do. They told me their sad story of wanting and trying, frustration and hopelessness.

I listened and explained that sometimes we can try too hard, whether it is trying to find the answer to a question or trying to be happy, sometimes trying hard has the opposite effect. Sometimes we just have to let go and stop trying, and things then occur naturally.

I told them that of the 135 million children born on the planet every year, most of them are born to mothers who are actively trying not to get pregnant.

In my world where language and words are all I have, the word 'TRY' implies failure. If I want someone to fail at a task I will tell them to try to do it and to find they cannot. This causes the brain to react in a strange, negative way and the task becomes impossible.

I told the couple about Milton Erickson's genius and explained that I was going to use Erickson's shock therapy. This of course created even more trepidation in the couple, and I quickly explained that it would not be painful for them, but it would be a shock.

This was straight out of Erickson's case with the uptight couple. I asked my clients to take a few minutes to decide before we proceeded, but reassured them that if they were brave enough to accept the treatment they would achieve their goal. The couple quickly agreed.

I then hypnotised them together with 'Parts Negotiation' therapy. I asked the part responsible for their ability to reproduce to make the changes at a molecular and cellular level that will enable the woman to conceive.

I suggested that they would remember the feeling they had for each other when they first met—the excitement, passion and love. I then told the couple to open their eyes and turn to face each other, which they did.

I asked them to think of the love they have for each other as they looked into each other's eyes, and to recall the early passion and pleasure that they had when making love with each other. The smiles on their faces and the look of love exchanged between the young couple will stay in my mind forever. I then gave them a post-hypnotic suggestion that whenever they lay together for the purpose of creating a new life that they would feel the passion and love that they are feeling now.

As they looked at each other I asked if they were ready for the shock treatment. Still smiling at each other they nodded their heads. I instructed the couple to close their eyes and to go deeper into hypnosis, which they did.

I then in a very authoritarian voice said, 'In a moment I will count to five, on "four" your eyes will open and on "five" you will feel a desire for each other stronger than you have ever felt before.' I counted, and on "five" their eyes opened and they turned toward each other and smiled. I then said (as Erickson had said to his clients), 'Now go home and fuck for fun and hope that you don't get pregnant too quickly.' I brought the couple out of hypnosis. The couple quickly said their goodbyes to me and left my office.

I received a letter of thanks from the couple, about six weeks later which read 'We are pregnant.' Eight months later I received another letter from the couple with a photo of their son Christopher, which I keep to this day.

Introduction to the Jacquin Arrow Technique.

Although I initially developed this technique to deal with long term chronic pain, what has become clear over the past few years is that this technique works not only for physical pain, but also for emotional pain, including anxiety, stress, grief and loss.

Here are a couple of examples from two very different cases of mine, in which I used the Arrow Technique, after which I explain how this technique was developed by me and then the steps of the technique so that you can use it to help others.

Case one: Deborah's Story

Over the years I have seen many seemingly miraculous and as yet, medically, unexplained changes in people by using hypnosis.

A client came to see me for help in losing weight. On meeting the lady, it was obvious that she was in pain. I asked if she was, although it was obvious, and she said she had a medical condition known as fibromyalgia, a condition in which the person suffers severe pain and discomfort throughout their body.

I asked the client if she would like to be free of the pain, explaining that as she was going to be with me for at least ninety minutes, I wanted her to be comfortable. She looked at me as if I were mad and said, 'What do you mean do I want to be free of the pain? Of course, I do, but I have had this condition for fourteen years and the doctors have told me that although I won't die from the condition, I will die with it.' They thought there was no cure or help that they could give other than painkillers—she was already taking 26 different pills a day.

Having listened to this sad story of negative medical suggestions, I asked the question again, 'Do you want to be free of the pain?' She said yes, so I ran the Arrow Technique. This technique was created by me and developed specifically to help people in pain, whether the pain be physical or emotional.

Having established using a scale of 1-10 how much pain the client was in (for her it was 9 at the time) I ran the technique. After approximately five minutes, the client had zero pain in her body and we continued with the session for weight loss.

A few days later the lady rang me to inform me that since the session she had felt none of the useless, unnecessary pain that she had been experiencing for the past fourteen years and her eating habits had changed already. Five months on from this call, the lady had lost five stone in weight and had gone from taking 26 painkillers a day to taking none. She said that her life had changed from that very first session.

Case Two: The Aggrieved Wife

Elton John sang the words of Bernie Taupin, '"Sorry" seems to be the hardest word'. There is I believe something harder to say than 'sorry', and that is 'I forgive you'. It has been said that it only takes a moment, and you only have to forgive someone once, yet resentment, anger and hate can last forever, and takes a lot of work to sustain.

The client in this story was a lady who came to see me for help in losing weight, but as in many cases I have seen, that was not the actual reason she had been put on my path. We spoke about her weight goals and what she wanted to achieve. She then told me her story and the reason she believed she had put on the weight that she now wanted to lose.

Ten years previously, she had just had a baby boy who at the time was just a few months old. She had started having sex again with her husband and discovered that he had given her a sexually transmitted disease. On questioning, her husband, he at first denied that he had had sex with anyone other than his wife. His wife persisted in her questioning and accusation, and eventually the husband admitted that he had been 'dogging', a term given to an activity where a group of strangers would park their cars in an isolated spot somewhere and then randomly have sex with whoever or whatever was in the cars. Man, woman or animal.

The woman divorced her husband and brought up her son on her own. The husband had nothing more to do with her or the child. He had given them no financial support; all he had left her with was a lifelong STD. The client was as you would expect very angry, and rightly so.

For the past ten years before she had come to see me, she had put on six stone in weight, she was taking pills for stress and anxiety and her poor child had had a miserable existence. She knew that her anger and hatred toward her ex was making her ill and more importantly making her son's life a misery, but she did not know what to do to change the situation. I suggested that she forgive her husband, this suggestion brought a tirade of venomous words aimed in my direction. She asked me loudly, 'Have you not been listening? Do you think what he did deserves forgiveness? Can't you see what he has done to me and my child?'

I answered her calmly, 'I can see what he has done to you, and I can't begin to know how you feel, but you haven't seen your ex for years and the chances are he is now doing to someone else what he did to you and he is not suffering in any way. You and your son are still suffering and whether you accept it or not it is the anger and resentment that you feel that is making you ill and your son's life miserable. You may believe that you have no choice, but I know that you have, and the choices are: to forgive your ex, or continue to suffer. You don't have to mean it, and you don't have to say it to his face, but you must do it so that you can move on.'

The client understandably protested that she could not. I reiterated my reason for suggesting why she should and that with the use of hypnosis we could together free her from the anger and pain she had been experiencing for far too long. Eventually she agreed, and with the use of Parts Negotiation we asked the part that was protecting her to find another way of keeping her and her son safe, that at the same time would allow her freedom from any irrational fear and anxiety. I then ran the Arrow Technique, loading all the hatred, anger and loathing into the target. In her mind, if not in her heart, the client forgave her ex, put down the hatred, anger and pain and regained her life, happiness and joy.

The Jacquin Arrow Technique

How The Arrow Technique Came To Be

Having worked with hypnosis since 1995, primarily for help with bad habits, smoking, alcohol, and drugs, I developed a fascination about the actual physical effects hypnosis can have on the body. Reading case studies written about Milton Erickson's patients, his words of genius remained with me on the subject of treating people in pain.

If you ask the general public what they think hypnosis is, the chances are that many would use the words 'relaxation' or 'sleep'. This belief that when a person is hypnotised they are relaxed or asleep comes from stage hypnosis videos and films that people have seen.

In reality, hypnosis has nothing to do with sleep or relaxation. Now if you have a client who is in serious pain the idea of suggesting that they relax is ludicrous. Erickson understood and enlightened the world of hypnosis with his understanding that hypnosis was a heightened focus of attention. He would ask his pain client to focus on the pain and to find the very centre of the pain and focus their attention on it, just for a moment.

He would then use this focus of attention to transition his client into trance.

Throughout my adult life I have from time to time suffered with kidney stones, a build-up of calcium in the kidneys that are like little bits of grit. This causes intense pain until they pass through your system or are broken down with medication.

Long before I knew anything about hypnosis, when I would experience this pain, and before I received pain relief medication, I developed a technique to help myself disassociate from the pain. I would remember a specific holiday that I had had in France with a girlfriend. We drove in her white Mazda sports car down through France to a place called Orbison.

On the way, we stopped by a river bank and had a picnic. This was my go-to memory in order to disassociate myself from intense pain.

I would try to remember the number plate of the car, the colour of my girlfriend's shorts, the make of the beer we drank and the kind of cheese and bread that we ate. The more focused I became on the memory, the further from the pain I could remove myself. It got to the point where I could go back to my body by the side of the road and experience it again, and look at myself at the present time, at this point I would experience complete freedom from the pain.

These two ideas had germinated in my mind and I put together an idea for a pain control technique—'The Arrow Technique'. In 2003, I ran a group smoking event in Wales at which 200 smokers attended. As I always did as the event ended, I told the audience that I would be back in six weeks and if they knew anyone who wanted to quit the habit or wanted any other hypnotherapy, to let them know.

A lady who had been attending the event asked if I could do anything for pain. I of course said yes. I asked who it was for and she said it was for her as she had been in pain for nine years. I told her that she didn't have to wait for six weeks until I returned and that if she waited until everyone had left I would help her. Another lady asked if she could stay as she had spondylosis (degeneration of the vertebrae in her spine) and had been on crutches for years because of her condition.

I said that of course she could stay. The room emptied apart from my assistants who were busy tidying the room, the aunt and son of the lady on crutches who were there to take her home, and the friend of the other woman was also present.

I sat the two women down and used one of the simple hypnotic inductions you have already learned in this book and ran for the first time what is now known as the Arrow Technique.

This intervention took no longer than ten minutes from the ladies sitting down to when they opened their eyes again. I looked at the women who had spondylosis and asked, 'Where has the pain gone now?' She looked at me with astonishment and replied, 'I don't have any pain, I cannot feel any pain.' With this the other lady started to cry. I asked her if she was alright and she replied, 'I have no pain. For the first time in nine years I have no pain.' She was crying tears of joy.

The lady with the crutches then stood up and asked me to hold her crutches for her. She then proceeded to walk tentatively toward me. I asked if she was in pain she replied, 'No, and I have not walked without crutches for twelve years.'

She then told me that she had an MRI scan coming up in the next week, and asked if I thought she should still go. I of course said yes and added that 'it would be nice to go for the scan with no pain'. She said, 'I will', then thanked me, took hold of her young son's hand and walked out of the conference room holding the crutches under her arm.

The other woman's pain had gone completely also. This was the first time I had used this technique and I really had no idea whether it would work or not, but the two women were in need of help and I was not charging them, so I ran the technique as if I had run it a thousand times.

Since then I have indeed run the technique thousands of times and I have taught others to do the same, and the results have been outstanding—some would say miraculous—for all who use it.

The Arrow Technique - Protocol

Ask the client to sit comfortably and close their eyes. Ask them to take a deep breath and as they exhale to allow their body to relax. Then give the following instructions.

(1) Imagine that you are drifting up out of your body and drifting way up high, leaving your body in the chair. Drifting higher and higher.

(2) Look down, and in your mind's eye, see a target, like an archery target, way down below you. A massive target, picture it in your mind's eye. Now in the very centre of the target is the pain that you were experiencing.

(3) In a moment I will make this sound: SWOOSH, and you will be fired, shot like an arrow right through the centre of the target into a space of total bliss. But I need you to be brave because as you pass through the target, you will experience the pain even more intensely for a moment, a millisecond, but be brave, THIS IS THE LAST TIME THIS USELESS, UNNECESSARY PAIN WILL EVER AFFECT YOU. So be brave, get ready... SWOOSH. And now you are through the target, just drifting in a space of total bliss. Nothing bothers or affects you, nothing disturbs you, just drifting in a space of bliss.

(4) Now I would like you to drift over to the other side of this room and see yourself from the other side of the room sitting in that chair. You can see the clothes that you are wearing, and you can hear my voice. Notice as you watch yourself that every ounce of that useless pain has gone from your body. You cannot feel it, you cannot experience it. The harder you try and remember what it felt like the further away it goes.

(5) Now I would like your unconscious mind to make the changes at a molecular, cellular level that will enable you to have complete freedom from the useless, unnecessary pain forever. So, go ahead, only when the unconscious mind has made the changes at a molecular, cellular level that will enable you to have complete freedom from the useless, unnecessary pain forever only then will you drift back over to your body, drop down into your body in that chair, unable to experience any of the useless, unnecessary pain ever again. Go ahead take your time, do it thoroughly.

(6) As soon as the client opens their eyes look directly at them and ask,
'WHERE HAS THE PAIN GONE NOW?

ON A SCALE OF ONE TO TEN, WHERE HAS THE PAIN GONE NOW?

TRY AND FIND IT AND FIND YOU CANNOT.'

(7) When the client struggles to find the pain, you say 'Good it will never affect you again. ENJOY.'

(8) Be amazed.

The Jacquin Time Machine Technique

I am not a great advocate of regression therapy as it is generally practiced, but there are times when I believe it would be of benefit to my client to reassess a past event.

I only ever do this with the client dissociated physically from the past event.

Below are a couple of examples of actual cases in which I helped a client overcome a past traumatic event, using this technique.

Case: Saying Goodbye

Sometimes people are placed on your path for what seems to be one reason and then you realise that that is not the reason they have met you. This was the case for the client in this story.

The lady came to see me to help her lose weight. Although she was not seriously overweight she felt she would be healthier and happier if she could lose 10 kilos (22 pounds). During the consultation and goal-setting part of the session, the lady was jovial and happy.

We discussed how the session would go and I allayed any doubts she may have had about the process of hypnosis and then I hypnotised her.

Approximately ten minutes into the hypnosis, the client started to cry and sob. I reassured her that whatever was causing the emotion or had caused the initial pain, she had survived, and I asked her to stay with the feeling, and examine what had caused it.
After a while she slowly stopped sobbing and I brought her out of the trance. I asked her if she wanted to discuss what had happened while she was in trance and she said no. We finished the session with some suggestions for weight loss and she left.

A week later she returned for a second appointment. I greeted her and asked how her weight loss was progressing. She looked me straight in the eyes as if seeing me for the first time and said, 'I realise now that is not why I am here.'

She told me that during our first session when she was in trance, a memory of an event that had happened when she was six years old had come to her clearly, a memory she thought she had buried years before.

She went on to say that looking back at her life she felt that this childhood experience had affected many of the decisions she had made throughout her life.

I asked her if she would share it with me and she proceeded to tell me that when she was six, her brother who was eleven at the time and two of his friends of the same age had (in her words) messed about with her, they hadn't raped her or anything as serious, but had touched her inappropriately.

She realised as she recalled this event that although she was now in her forties, she had never been close to her brother and she had never let her two sons stay with him. She told me that when she in her twenties she had questioned her brother about the incident and he had told her that he had no recollection of it.

I explained that there was a theory that up until about the age of sixteen years old, if a child has an experience that is too traumatic or painful for them to deal with, the mind can bury it or push it to the back of their mind (this I believe is a cause of panic attacks, but that is a discussion for later on in this book). I told her that this could be the reason that her brother had no recollection of the incident.

I explained that we could deal with the problem, but it may be painful.

She said that she would agree to do anything to resolve this. I explained that I would use my method of regression therapy—which did not involve weeks or hours of therapy, but minutes—and if she did this she would be free of the underlying hurt and mistrust that she had had for over thirty years.

I then hypnotised her and used the method that I call the 'Jacquin Time Machine'. I asked her unconscious to allow her to go through time as if time no longer existed, back to the very first moments that related to the problem.

I told her to go back with all the understanding, strength and experience that she had now, as a mother, a woman and an adult.

I said that knowing she had survived it, she was to be brave and this would be the last time this would ever affect her. I then ran the technique.

I told her to drop down beside her young self and walk the child through the event, to take the learnings and strengths from the event and store them in her mind and then let go of the emotion attached to the event—any pain, embarrassment or sadness.

I asked her to reassess the event as an adult with all the understanding she had now as a mother. I told her that when she was ready to free herself forever, she was to give the child a hug, thank her for going through that horrible experience for her, tell her that she had survived it, then give the child a hug and a kiss and say goodbye.

I told her to step over the line into her future, to turn around and see that beautiful little girl with a smile on her face, waving goodbye. I told her to close the door behind her, and leave the past where it belongs—in the past—as she moved on with her life, free of the past, free to be. I then brought the client out of the trance.

The client reported that on visiting the incident again as an adult, with the understanding that she now had as a mother, her perspective had changed. She saw her brother clearly, as an eleven-year-old child. As it happened her sons were eleven and thirteen at the time she visited me, so I asked her the question, 'If one of your boys did something stupid or crazy, no matter how bad it was, would you hold it against them forever?' She answered no. I asked, 'why not?' She said it was because they are only eleven and thirteen, and kids do stupid things.

This realisation and the use of hypnosis to reassess and let go of the negative emotion attached to the past event changed this client's life. Her relationship with her brother changed and she and her sons visited him often where he lived in France, and she never ever mentioned the incident again to him. Furthermore, over the next weeks after our time together, she lost ten kilos.

The Jacquin Time Machine Technique - Protocol

(1) Hypnotise the client.

(2) Tell them that the chair they are sitting in is a time machine and that when you click your fingers that they will be sucked back through time as if time doesn't exist, back to the very first moment that relates to the problem.

(3) Ask their unconscious to allow them to go through time as if time no longer existed, back to the very first moments that related to the problem, but to go back with all the understanding, strength and experience that they have now, as a mother or father, woman or man, an adult.

(4) As soon as they are back to the event in their mind, instruct them to drop down beside their young self and walk them through the event to take the learnings and strengths from the event and store them in their mind and then let go of the emotion attached to the event—any pain, embarrassment or sadness. Instruct the client to reassess the event as an adult with all the understanding they have now.

(5) When they have done this and are ready to free themselves forever, give their younger self a hug, thank them for going through the horrible experience for you.

(6) Tell their younger self that you survived, tell them anything else that they need to know for them to be the best adult they can be. Then give their younger self a hug and a kiss and say goodbye.

(7) Step over the line into your future. Turn around and see their younger self with a smile on their face waving goodbye as you free them forever, and then close the door behind you.

(8) Leave all the hurt, pain, sadness and fear where it belongs, in the past.

(9) Bring the client out of hypnosis, keeping all the learning and strength.

Psychological and Physiological Anchoring

This is the ability to anchor a feeling or emotion with a physical action.

The technique known as 'anchoring' is as with most psychological techniques taken from nature (something that we do naturally or unconsciously, that has been studied and developed as a conscious ability or skill). It is a very powerful, simple technique.

If you have children, then you are already anchoring feelings with them, probably without knowing. You will be anchoring feelings with your partner and your friends and if you are a teacher or coach you will be anchoring feelings with your student.

If your child hurts themselves and you comfort them with a hug or a kiss and a kind word, and you do this throughout their childhood, then the chances are that even when as an adult your child is hurt whether emotionally or physically and you give them a hug or a kiss and you take the same tone of voice that you used when they were young, they will feel reassured or comforted. This is what I mean by 'anchoring a feeling'.

In the 1970s, Richard Bandler and John Grinder believed that by studing people who excelled in what they did and modeling their actions and mental attitude the success could be replicated. The first three people that they modelled were therapists. In studying these people, they realised that they were anchoring feelings with their clients unconsciously. They found that they could anchor empowering, positive resources within their clients consciously.

A summary of how this is done follows after a couple of very different cases in which I used the anchoring technique. Once learned you will not only be able to help others, but also empower yourself.

The Therapy Session That Worked Too Well

A young couple came to see me seeking my help to them stop smoking, which I helped them do within one session.

Two weeks later the wife came back having made an appointment on another matter. She told me that her husband and she had been having problems in their sexual relationship.

It had gotten to the point where the only way they could have sex was for them both to use cocaine as a stimulant. Neither of them wanted to continue in this manner, which is why the wife had made the appointment to see me.

She explained that the initial cause of the problem was her inability to experience an orgasm whilst making love with her husband, and she hoped that I could help. I asked her if she had ever experienced an orgasm. She told me that although she had never experienced it with a partner, she could by fantasising and masturbation. As hypnosis and the hypnotic state relies heavily on the use of the imagination this was helpful to know and gave me great hope that I could help her utilising the anchoring technique.

This of course meant that in order to install the anchor she would have to experience an orgasm herself. I instructed the client in how to install an anchor and how to use self-hypnosis, using confidence as an example.

Through the utilisation of the hypnotic state in which the senses are heightened and the ability to use the imagination increased, this was accomplished in her own home, and the experience and feeling was anchored into her hand by squeezing a finger and thumb together and repeating what was to be her trigger word. The client contacted me about a week later by text, with this amusing message.

"Thank you so much for your help in helping me achieve the pleasure that had been missing from my sexual relationship with my husband. Don't be surprised though if you get a call from my husband asking you to tone it down a bit. Regards."

Anchoring For Personal Change

The Anchoring Technique - Protocol

Choose the resourceful feeling or emotion that you want to anchor so as to be able to utilise it at any time. For example, confidence, fearlessness, determination, etc.

(1) You must set a physical anchor. This can be as simple as crossing your fingers or squeezing a finger and thumb together.

(2) Set a trigger word—one word that you will use specifically to trigger the resourceful feeling.

(3) Elicit the feeling. This is done by remembering a time when you have felt the feeling strongly and then re-establishing the feeling by the use of breathing, posture and internal dialogue.

(4) Adopt the posture you were in when you felt the feeling strongly in the past.

(5) Breathe how you breathed when you experienced the feeling strongly in the past. Say what you said to yourself when you experienced the feeling strongly in the past (internal dialogue).

(6) When you are experiencing the empowering feeling that you want, you anchor it by applying the physical anchor that you decided on and repeating the trigger word to yourself. You continue to do this as you are experiencing the feeling at its strongest and hold the anchor on for 8-10 seconds whilst repeating the trigger word.

Repeat Step 6 three times, each time endeavouring to experience the feeling even stronger than before.

The anchor will now be set, and anytime that you need to feel the resourceful feeling again, you just use the physical anchor and the trigger word.

Now that you know how to hypnotise, when you run this technique with a client or a friend, use the "Power Anchor Technique" as described below.

Power Anchor Technique

Ask your client to choose the resourceful feeling or emotion that they want to anchor—confidence, fearlessness, determination, etc.

Explain how you will do this by describing the steps of the technique. Get an agreement that they understand their role.

Begin by hypnotising the client.

Elicit the desired feeling/resource by encouraging them to breathe as they did when they experienced the feeling in the past, to say what they said to themselves when they experienced the feeling and as closely as they can to adopt the posture they were in when they experienced the feeling.

Watch for the client to place the physical anchor on, then encourage them to repeat the trigger word in their mind as they continue to experience the empowering feeling.

You count silently to 8 as they do this and on the count of 8 ask the client to let go of the anchor and open their eyes.

Repeat the above steps, twice more, each time encouraging the client to experience the feeling even more intensely.

On the third round of this technique as you see the client place the anchor on, you give the post hypnotic suggestion, 'From today whenever you place the anchor on and repeat the trigger word in your mind, you will immediately return to this feeling.'

Repeat this suggestion three times rapidly.

Ask the client to let go of the anchor and open their eyes.

Anchoring is probably the greatest gift you can give to anyone who wants to perform at their best, whether it be in business, sports, sales or the bedroom.

On the next two pages are few examples from my experience in working with various performers.

The Squash Player

The very first anchor that I set was for a friend who played squash at county level, but had two rivals that he could not beat. At the time I was only studying hypnosis and was devouring every book on NLP and hypnosis. My friend was a bricklayer and I met him in his lunch hour and did the hypnosis and anchor in the cab of his pickup truck.

I saw him a few days later and he told me how on the previous two evenings he had played against both men. He told how the first player became so frustrated with the beating he was taking on the squash court, that at one point he actually threw his racket down. The second player hardly won a point off my friend. This proved to him and me that without any extra physical training or skill, you can achieve incredible things when you set your mind correctly.

The Cyclist

A veteran cyclist (over 35 years old) came to see me because he was finding it difficult to stay focused when the road races he was competing in were over 50 kilometres (30 miles) long. He told about how his mind would start to wander and this would slow him down.

His P.B. (personal best) position was fifth in the UK championships, which he had achieved only once. I asked him to bring his race bike into my office and got him to sit on it.

I hypnotised him and encouraged him to get into an incredibly powerful state of focus and determination. When he was in this heightened state we set a physical anchor into his handle bars and he repeated the words of his favourite rock song in his mind as his audio trigger. We did this exercise three times. The following weekend he competed against the very best cyclist in the UK and came first.

The Football Star

A young man came to see me because his lack of confidence was jeopardising his career. When I enquired what he did for a living, he told me he was a footballer playing for Millwall FC who were playing in the first division at the time. My client told me that he was not being picked for the team, because of his anxiety and confidence issues. To help him I used trance and anchoring to place a feeling of confidence into his hand. I only worked with him once. He got back into the team and the team got to the final that year of the FA cup, playing the Premier division champions: Manchester United. My client played in every match leading up to and including the final and it was the best result the club had ever had.

The MMA Fighter

I was asked to work with the UK's number one heavy weight MMA (mixed martial arts) star. This man, when out of the ring, was an accomplished writer, gentleman and loving family man. In the fight cage, he would unleash the 6'5" 17 stone (196cm 108kg/240lb) single-minded, unfeeling, fighting-machine man mountain that he had honed and crafted in the gym. These two very real sides of his personality created a very good life for himself and his family.

The problem was that every now and then, the kind, gentleman, writer, philosopher part of him would interfere in the ring, and the brutal, monstrous fighter would interfere in his family and social life. He didn't need the fighter to think, he knew he could rely on the fact that he had worked his body and honed the unconscious skills in the gym and all he needed to do was unleash the fighter and he would do the job. More important, he didn't need the cruel, unfeeling monster in his family life. With the use of an anchor and hypnosis, fixing this was accomplished.

The anchor was this: When he was in the ring he would bang his gloves together three times hard and repeat the word 'win' and as he did so, the gentleman, father, writer and philosopher would step out of the ring. When the fight was over, and his gloves were removed the monster stayed in his cage, until called upon to fight again. This successfully changed his ability in the ring and his family life out of the ring.

The Super-Bike Motorcycle Rider

I was asked by a Super-Bike team owner to work with their team rider. The rider was super fit, dedicated to his sport, fearless and naturally talented. but for whatever reason could not finish in better than thirteenth place in his league. He was highly intelligent individual. He had been racing motorcycles since he was a boy. I explained that he didn't have to be involved consciously in riding his bike, because he had trained his unconscious to race for him. He totally understood this. We anchored a feeling into his racing crash helmet that enabled him to separate his conscious mind from his unconscious and let his unconscious race for him. He finished fifth which was his best result to that date. He reported than while he was on the track travelling at 160 mph he had had time to notice the faces of the people watching the race.

Self Hypnosis

Self-hypnosis is a natural trance state that enables you to eliminate negative or limiting behaviours, change any of your behaviours and even change your physical being.

There are many ways of entering a trance state safely by yourself. The two described below are, in my opinion, the easiest and most effective.

Imagine that everything you believe you are is just an opinion and not real.

As I have stated often throughout this book, hypnosis and trance are natural states. My understanding is that every emotion, behaviour or unconscious ability is just a trance—some positive and life-enhancing, others negative and destructive. With this understanding and the ability to self-hypnotise, you can go into hypnosis and create a positive emotion or ability, or, and here is the greatest understanding, you can eliminate any negative emotion or behaviour.

There are different ways to take yourself into hypnosis. One of the best ways when you first start out as a hypnotist is to record a progressive induction and then listen to it yourself. Within the recording you can give suggestions to yourself for the things you want to achieve in your life. This will also embed the induction into your mind so that when you use it you will be more confident and proficient.

When you are working with your client, once they are in hypnosis you can give the post-hypnotic suggestion for self-hypnosis and anchor this to a word. All of my clients have the ability to use self-hypnosis and they do this by sitting comfortably and repeating the word 'relax' four times to themselves.

When entering hypnosis by yourself there are a couple of rules that I give to my clients and also follow myself.

1) Always state your desired outcome in the positive, for example 'I want to be well' as opposed to 'I don't want to be ill', 'I want to be successful' as opposed to 'I don't want to fail'.
2) State a length of time for you to be in trance. If you don't state a time you will not get stuck in hypnosis, but you may drift off into sleep. At any time during the self-hypnosis you can bring yourself out by counting from 1 to 5.

Here are another couple of ways of entering the hypnotic state by yourself: you can listen to the audio session in which I give a post-hypnotic suggestion for entering trance by repeating a certain word. You can enter trance whenever and wherever you may be, providing you have taken the time to enter trance a few times before and given yourself a post-hypnotic suggestion for entering trance instantly.

Firstly, find a quiet place where you will be undisturbed for a while.
Sit or lay comfortably (keep your arms and legs by your side). Take a breath in and as you exhale allow your eyes to close. Relax the muscles around your eyes and continue to do so until you feel that they are so relaxed they just won't work. When you feel you have reached that point of relaxation you can test by trying to open your eyes. If they are so relaxed you cannot open them, if not keep relaxing your eyes until you reach that point.
Allow the feeling of relaxation to spread down through the rest of your body until you feel that you just cannot move.
Think about the people you love and feel that love.

Now you are ready to self-suggest.

Anchoring The Trance State

With the understanding that you now have of anchoring, you can utilize the technique to enter the trance state rapidly. All you have to do is to anchor it.

After using the technique above, when you feel as relaxed as you possibly can, anchor the feeling with a word and a physical action. Repeat this two more times. Then whenever you feel the need to enter the trance state you can just use the anchor.

Revivification

A simple and elegant way to induce a trance is known as 'revivification'. You revive an experience of trance by thinking of a past experience you have had in which you found yourself drifting as a mind.

Not sure when this has happened? Have you ever been on a train journey, looking out of the window watching the scenery passing by as your mind drifts to another space and time? Have you ever been so engrossed in a book that an hour has passed without you realising?

These are both examples of trance that can be revivified to induce a trance state in the present moment. This is a very useful technique.

Revivification can be used for different goals. The example below is for dissociating from physical discomfort or pain.

To utilise revivification to create trance, direct your thoughts toward experiences where a naturalistic trance occurs.

To utilise revivification to utilise resources, direct your thoughts toward experiences where those resources were at play.

Once you have found an area with resourceful states associated into it, begin to ask questions in a specific way to gather increasing amount of detail. The more you get into the specific details of the memory, the deeper the internal search becomes, the deeper you go into the revived trance and the further away from wakeful awareness you will drift.

How we recall the past event that we are revivifying can alter the ways in which we use this technique.

Disassociated memories are when we remember a past experience and we see ourselves in the event doing whatever it was we did we are disassociated from experiencing the memory.

Associated memories are when we remember a past experience and we feel what we felt at the time of the event we are associated in the memory and experiencing the memory as if it were now.

Distancing Yourself from Physical Pain

This technique can be an extremely good way to separate yourself from physical pain. Follow through the steps below and notice how at the end you are no longer concentrating on the pain that was sapping your energy.

Remember a past event, maybe a wedding or a family occasion. Associate into the memory so that you can experience it again in the first person. Put yourself back into the event.

Firstly, remember as many people as you can who were there. What were they wearing? What sort of hairstyles did they have?

Then think about the weather. What sort of day was it? Was there a breeze or was it perfectly calm? How hot was it? Did it feel fresh or humid?

Think about the setting. Were you inside or outside? What sort of plants were there? What was the décor like? What was the furniture like?

Think about the sounds. Were people talking, shouting, laughing or crying? Was there any music?

Can you see any vehicles? How many were there? What makes? What colours?

See the faces of more people, maybe someone you love—see their smile, hear their voice, remember what they said and how they said it.

Become more detailed. What sort of car were you driving at the time? What was the registration number? What colour was it? What did the seats feel like?

Become more and more detailed. See what you saw, hear what you heard, and feel what you felt.

As you do this, you will notice that you have been paying less and less attention to your physical feelings in the present to the extent that any pain you were experiencing vanishes from your mind.

Parts Negotiation + Rewind Visualisation to Overcome Phobias

The following technique has many names. As with nearly all hypnosis techniques, the component parts have been used in some form or other, probably for centuries.

If you are familiar with NLP (neuro-linguistic programming) you may recognise the format. The theory behind this technique is that every thought or memory has certain elements involved. These are known as sub-modalities.

If you think of a past event, that memory will be made up of pictures, sounds, and even smells. Each of these components has sub-modalities, such as with the visual aspect being pictures. Some sub-modalities are:

Movement: (fast, slow, static)
Colours: (black and white, colours, bright, dim)
Sounds: (loud, quiet, high, low)
Olfactory: (sweet, sour, nice, nasty)

As an equation it may look like this:

pictures + sounds + olfactory = feelings and emotions

These pictures, sounds and so on—the sub-modalities—are the components that create the memory.

If we change any of the sub-modalities, we can change the feelings and emotions attached to that memory. For instance, let us imagine we are speaking to a client that has suffered a traumatic event. If we ask them to recall the event and ask about the sub-modalities and the picture they see is clear, in colour and moving, and the sounds are loud. By getting the client to change the picture to a still photograph instead of a movie, changing the picture from colour to black-and-white and changing the sound from loud to soft, you will change the feelings and emotions they have about the event.

As with all of my work I try and remove the complexity or as I like to call it the 'fluff' that many techniques have, and get down to the nuts and bolts of what actually does the work.

My son likes to call this particular guided visualisation, 'Room 101' a reference to the George Orwell, novel '1984', in which room 101 housed all of your worst fears.

So here are the steps for this technique as used with a spider phobia but of course if the object of the phobia can be placed in the room, you just change the words to suit.

Hypnotise the client.

Script

You are sitting in an empty cinema.

Looking up at a blank screen.

You are sitting in an empty cinema.

Looking up at a blank screen.

Drift up out of your body, and up to the room where the camera is, at the back of the cinema.

Now look down and see yourself sitting in the chair, watch yourself looking up at the blank screen.

You can see the movie camera.

Click it on and see a picture of yourself on the screen. You are standing outside of a room. There are a set of closed, double doors that lead into the room.

Remember that this is just a film and you are just going to watch yourself watching it.

In a moment when I say, you will press the start button and run the movie.

Remember that this is just a film and you are just going to watch yourself watching it.

Press the start button and watch yourself on the screen opening the doors and walking into the room.

Remember that this is just a film and you are just going to watch yourself watching it.

In the room there are spiders hanging from the ceiling, they are on the furniture and floor.

This is just a film and you are just going to watch yourself watching it.

Watch yourself walking through the room.

You can see the spiders in the room as you watch yourself walking through the room.

Remember that this is just a film and you are just watching it.

As you watch the film you can see that there is a door on the other side of the room.

Watch yourself walk out of those doors and close the doors behind you, safe and sound.

Stop the film.
Now press rewind and rewind the film quickly so everything is going backwards. Swoosh until once again you are watching a still picture of yourself outside those double doors.

In a moment you are going to run the film again, but this time as a cartoon. Everything in the room will be cartoon like.

Start the film.

Watch yourself walking into the room. There are cartoon spiders hanging from the ceiling. You can see their funny little hairy legs. Some of them are wearing little boots and funny hats. You can hear their funny little voices.

Watch them as you see yourself walking through the room. Some of the spiders are dancing and some are playing little instruments.

Watch yourself walk through the room and out of the door on the other side. Watch yourself closing the door behind you, safe and sound.

Stop the film.

Rewind the film, swoosh, and see yourself once again outside the room by those double doors.

In a moment you are going to run the film again, but this time as a cartoon and I want you to put some cartoon or funny music to it. Everything in the room will be cartoon-like and you will hear that music in your mind.

Start the film.

Watch yourself walking into the room. You can hear that music. There are cartoon spiders hanging from the ceiling.

You can see their funny little hairy legs. Hear that music.

Some of the spiders are wearing little boots and funny hats. You can hear their funny little voices, singing that Looney Tune.

Watch them as you see yourself walking through the room. Some of the spiders are dancing and some are playing little instruments, hear the music.

Watch yourself walk through the room and out of the door on the other side. Watch yourself closing the door behind you, safe and sound.

Stop the film.

Rewind the film, swoosh, and see yourself once again outside the room by those double doors.

Now drop back into your body in the chair in the cinema. Walk up to the 'you' on the screen and thank them for doing that for you.

Now pull them into you so that they become a part of you once again and from today no matter how hard you try, you will never experience that fear again. The harder you try to remember how it felt to be afraid of spiders the further away that feeling goes.

No matter how hard you try, you will never feel that fear again.

Jacquin Phobia Technique:

Another phobia technique—this one created, designed and developed by me—is the Jacquin Phobia Technique, which utilises Rapid-Eye Movement. It has been used in many ways with great effect.

As I have stated, there are two problems that I 'symptom scale': fear and pain. This technique uses the scan as a starting point in the actual protocol. This will become clear shortly. Below is the description of how I use this. You of course can play with it, adjust it and embellish it in whatever way you feel fit.

Hypnotise the client.

Ask them to see the number that they scaled the problem at (for the purpose of this example only, we will assume they symptom-scaled it as an 'eight').

See the number eight in your mind's eye. Picture it, colour it in your mind.

Now see it moving from side to side, watch it move, speed it up, now slow it down. Now move it into the distance, watch it get smaller and smaller. Now bring it close so that it is huge. Now watch as it morphs into the number seven.

See the number seven. Move it from side to side, watch it move, speed it up, now slow it down. Now move it into the distance, watch it get smaller and smaller. Now bring it close so that it is huge. Now watch as it morphs into the number six.

See that number six. Move it from side to side, watch it move, speed it up, now slow it down. Now move it into the distance, watch it get smaller and smaller. Now bring it close so that it is huge. Now watch as it morphs into the number five.

See that number five. Move it from side to side, watch it move, speed it up, now slow it down. Now move it into the distance, watch it get smaller and smaller. Now bring it close so that it is huge. Now watch as it morphs into the number four.

See the number four. Move it from side to side, watch it move, speed it up, now slow it down. Now move it into the distance, watch it get smaller and smaller. Now bring it close so that it is huge. Now watch as it morphs into the number three.

See the number three. Move it from side to side, watch it move, speed it up, now slow it down. Now move it into the distance, watch it get smaller and smaller. Now bring it close so that it is huge. Now watch as it morphs into the number two.

See that number two. Move it from side to side, watch it move, speed it up, now slow it down. Now move it into the distance, watch it get smaller and smaller. Now bring it close so that it is huge. Now watch as it morphs into the number one.

See the number one. Move it from side to side, watch it move, speed it up, now slow it down. Now move it into the distance, watch it get smaller and smaller. Now bring it close so that it is huge. Now watch as it morphs into a zero.

See that zero. Move it from side to side, watch it move, speed it up, now slow it down. Now move it into the distance, watch it get smaller and smaller. Now bring it close so that it is huge.

Now step through that zero into a place of safety and calm. As you do that every irrational thought, every irrational fear disappears from your mind, never to affect you again. From today the harder you try and remember what it was like to be afraid or anxious the further away the fear and anxiety goes. No matter how hard you try, you will never feel that fear again.

Give positive suggestions and in your own time end the session.

The moment the client opens their eyes, look at them and ask, 'Where has the fear gone now? Try and feel it and find that you cannot. On a scale of one to ten where has the fear gone now?'

This technique can be used for fear, anxiety, loss or any other negative emotion that can be scaled. This is also a very effective self-hypnosis technique for rapidly changing any anxious feeling you may be having.

Although this technique can be used as an induction I tend to use it in the therapeutic encounter as a demonstration of the power of the mind and the imagination.

I will explain in detail exactly what I mean and how I apply it, but for now let me teach you the induction.

Rather than just read the instructions, I would prefer that you follow them, and if you do this, you should experience what your hypnotic subject will experience when you do this with them.

Obviously because you are reading this you will keep your eyes open rather than close them when asked in the written induction below, but stay with the instructions and you will have an experience of eyes-open hypnosis.

When you run this technique with someone you intend to hypnotise they will have your voice to guide them through it, so they can have their eyes closed.

Below is an actual phobia case in which I used it.

<u>The Chief Inspector of Police</u>

Interviews are one of the most stressful experiences we can go through, and the client in this case had tried and failed twice to achieve the next grade in his police career. The problem he was having was that at the interview the men interviewing him were his superiors and dressed accordingly in their dress uniforms. They sat higher than him in an attempt to intimidate and place him in a servile position, all of which had worked in the previous two interviews.

As with many uniformed groups, such as the army, navy and nursing, part of the training and indoctrination included intimidation by an authority figure which was creating a disproportionate respect and fear of superiors. He had throughout his years in the police force learned this. Although now a high-ranking officer himself, he still felt this fear of his superiors.

.

I treated this in exactly the same way as I deal with any other phobia, but with one twist. Whilst he was in hypnosis I had him visualise the interview as if he were watching the event on a screen and asked him to run it like a film, to the end. I then asked him to run it again, but this time see the men that were interviewing him as naked—no uniforms. I could see by his face that he was doing this in his mind. I asked him to run the film again with the naked interviewers, but to also add some funny music to the film. Once again, he began to smile as he did this. I gave him some very direct suggestions for fearlessness in the interview, and then brought him out of hypnosis.

The client reported back to me that during the interview he had felt completely different than he had before the hypnosis. When he was being interviewed he saw the men interviewing him for what they were—just men, no better or worse than he. He had spoken calmly, fearlessly and with authority throughout the interview, and he justifiably got the promotion that he had long deserved.

Child Dental Phobia Technique

Here is a technique used for a child with a dental phobia.

Another great way to help children with a phobia is to run the rewind technique described below. Once again, although everyone is capable of benefiting from this technique, children are particularly adept because of their ability to imagine. You will see why this is so important as we go through the technique.

Rewind Phobia Technique for Dental and Needle Phobia

Notice that the object of the phobic response can be changed to whatever the client is afraid of: dogs, spiders, snakes, clowns, etc.

Protocol

Hypnotise the client.

You are sitting in an empty cinema, looking up at a blank screen.

Drift up into the room where the camera is. Look down through the little window and watch yourself, watching the screen.

Switch the camera on and see a still photograph of you on the screen. You are standing by a closed door that leads into a big room.

Remembering that you are just watching a film on the screen and that you are safe in the camera room, click the camera on and start the film.

Watch yourself on the screen opening the door and walking into the room. The room is a dental surgery, you can see the dentist and the dental nurse. Watch as you see yourself walk over to the dentist chair and sit down. This is just a film and you are just watching it. You can see the dentist opening your mouth and you can see the needle. This is just a film and you are just watching it. You can see the examination taking place, you can hear the drill. Watch as the dentist finishes the work and watch yourself walk out of the door on the other side of the room, safe and sound. Stop the film.
Press rewind on the camera and watch the film rewind back to the start really quickly, everything moving backward.
Zzzzzzzzzzzzzzzzzzzzzzzzip.

Once again you can see yourself on the screen standing outside the door leading into the dentist's room.

Run the film again, but this time as a cartoon: everyone and everything in the room except you is a cartoon character. Start the film.

Watch yourself walking into the room. The dentist is a cartoon character and the nurse is a cartoon character. You can see their funny faces and funny ears and can hear their funny voices. Remember this just a film and you are just watching it. You can see the cartoon needle made of rubber, hear the funny sound of the drill, and watch as you sit in the chair and have the work done by those cartoon characters.

Watch yourself once again walking out of the doors on the other side of the room closing the door behind you, safe and sound. Stop the film.

Press rewind on the camera and watch the film rewind back to the start really quickly, everything moving backward. Zzzzzzzzzzzzzzzzzzzzzzzip.

Once again you can see yourself on the screen standing outside the door leading into the dentist's room.

Run the film once again as a cartoon, everyone and everything in the room except you is a cartoon character, but this time you can hear some Looney Tunes music playing. Start the film.

Watch yourself walking into the room. The dentist is a cartoon character and the nurse is a cartoon character. Hear the music, see their funny faces and funny ears and listen to their funny voices as the Looney Tunes music plays.

Remember this just a film and you are just watching it. You can see the cartoon needle made of rubber, hear the funny sound of the drill, and watch as you sit in the chair and have the work done by those cartoon characters. Watch yourself once again, walking out of the doors on the other side of the room, closing the door behind you, safe and sound. Stop the film.

Press rewind on the camera and watch the film rewind back to the start really quickly, everything moving backward. zzzzzzzzzzzzzzzzzzzzzzzzzip.

Once again you can see yourself on the screen standing outside the door leading into the dentist's room.

Now drop down out of the camera room back into your body in the cinema seat. Go up to that younger you on the screen and thank them for doing that for you and then pull them into you so that they become part of you once again.
Now from today you will never experience that irrational fear and anxiety again. The harder you try to remember how it felt to be afraid the further away that fear will go. From today no matter how hard you try you will never experience that fear again.

"..I know that you will be happily unconcerned, unable to remember to be afraid. Now you can enter every situation knowing that you are protected".

<u>"Notice that throughout this technique that you keep reassuring the client that this is just a film that they are watching. Keep your description words to 'see' and 'hear'— NEVER 'feel'."</u>

Metaphor and Indirect Suggestion

If you are a student of hypnosis, the chances are that you will have heard reference to 'indirect suggestions'.

What is an indirect suggestion and why give an indirect suggestion instead of a direct suggestion?

Well, here are my thoughts on the subject.

As human beings we tend not to like to be told what to do. If I was to suggest that you make me a coffee, you may have a certain amount of resistance to doing it. If on the other hand I was to say that we have some really nice coffee in the cupboard and I really fancy some, then you are more likely to ask if I would like some and then make it for me.

When we communicate we often use analogy or stories to get a point across.

When someone is telling us a story or analogy in conversation, we assume there must be a reason that they are telling it. Our mind goes on an unconscious search for meaning. This is generally done out of our conscious awareness. Therefore, the intended point, the meaning, tends to be accepted with little or no resistance.

You could look at nearly all fairy stories in this way and, depending on your beliefs, you could look again at the stories in the Bible and see them in a new light as wonderful metaphors.

Milton Erickson was one of the greatest storytellers. He would often start a hypnotherapy session with the words, 'My friend John', and then he would tell a story. The client would often wonder when the therapy would start, just as the session was finishing. They would then find their problem gone.

Erickson knew exactly what he was doing with his words at all times.

In my work as a hypnotherapist, I will use metaphor in some form in every first session. Some I have learned and some I have created myself. Although I have seen tens of thousands of clients, I have only a handful of metaphors that I generally use.

How can you use the same metaphor with countless different problems and still get a result? The reason is that even in a group session with two hundred clients, each individual will do their own search for meaning and match that meaning to the resolution of their problem. This is the beauty of metaphor.

Here is one of my favourite metaphors which I have used many times for clients who feel they have to be perfect at everything. I found of variation of this in the book Hypnotherapy Scripts by Ronald Havens.

"I don't know if you know anything about the Navaho, Native American Indians. They weave these beautiful rugs. The colours are fantastic, and the designs are beautiful. They have been weaving these rugs for thousands of years. In each rug though they leave a minute knot and imperfection, and they do this on purpose.

'When they are asked why they leave that knot in the rug, their answer is the same as it has been for thousands of years.

'They say they leave that knot, that imperfection, so that the gods don't think they are trying to be God themselves.'

The rule is that you never try to explain the meaning of the metaphor, because everyone will extract their own meaning from it.

The Havens book is full of great metaphors and you can use stories from your own experiences if you think they suit the situation. If you are going to use metaphor/storytelling in your therapeutic work, say it with meaning and passion.

Metaphor: Girl on the train:

Here is another technique in the form of a metaphor I created for saying goodbye. I have used this, many times.

Below is one case to illustrate how I use it. As with all metaphor work that I do, it will be part of a more comprehensive intervention, generally embedded within a parts negotiation.

Judith's Story

Judith, a 38-year-old medical doctor, had asked for my help because of her crippling lack of confidence and low self-esteem. This had affected every aspect of her life, but now, as a happily married women with two sons of eight and ten years old, she was determined that it was not going to affect her family any more. Judith explained that she had a wonderful childhood and was brought up by loving parents. She was a brilliant academic and had gone to one of the UK's top universities.

At university she met David and for the first time in her life she experienced the feeling of being 'in love'. The relationship lasted for nearly a year before David began to see other women. As happens so often in the case of infidelity, the man, rather than be honest and take responsibility for his own weakness and accept that his needs lay beyond what he could get from a monogamous relationship, blamed his partner, who in this instance was Judith.

For more than six months he convinced Judith that it was her lack of beauty, sexual performance and personality that had made him sleep with other women. As with so many women who are in love, she believed him.

Remember how I said you could hypnotise someone? Create an emotion and give a suggestion. Remember that I said the majority of hypnotists are not 'Hypnotists', but are unaware that they are using hypnosis.

Well, David was one such person. He had, by continually creating heightened emotions within Judith and suggesting that she was ugly and uninteresting, creating a state of mind in Judith in which she accepted these continuous suggestions and they became her beliefs.

Now here she was fifteen years later, married to John, a wonderful man that loved her, with two beautiful children that adored her and yet still she was affected by an eighteen-month disastrous relationship that she had at university.

Having listened to Judith's sad story, I decided to run my 'Train Journey' metaphor.

Hypnotise the client and start whatever your preferred intervention is. At an appropriate time within your therapy session, start the metaphor.

'You are standing on an empty railway station platform, one of those old stations that you see out in the countryside. An old train pulls into the station, one of those trains with the slam doors. You open the train door and get into an empty carriage. As you sit down you notice that by your feet there are two big suitcases. The train pulls out of the station and moves down the track. As the train pulls into the next station you notice a man standing on the platform and as your carriage stops beside the man, you recognise the face, you know the smile. The man gets into your carriage and sits opposite you and when he speaks you know the voice.

The train pulls out of the station and moves along the track. The man's face, smile and especially his voice spikes you with a pain from long ago but not forgotten. I want you to be brave and do this and you will free yourself forever. Do this now: lean over to the man and thank him for any love that you shared, any pleasure that you had together and tell him that you forgive him.

Now in those two large suitcases is all the hurt, pain, sadness, embarrassment and every angry word and negative limiting belief he had left you with. The weight of all of this had been slowing you down and holding you back. Now push those suitcases over to the man, notice the weight of them, just how heavy all the doubts that were placed on you, were.

As you do this the train pulls into the next station. Open the door and let him out of the carriage, dragging those two suitcases with him. Slam the door behind him. As the train starts to move, you can still see that face clearly but as the train picks up speed the face gets smaller and now you cannot see that face, you cannot remember the voice or the smile and the harder you try the further away they go.

As the train moves along the track you close your eyes and picture a figure, hunched over, straining to walk as he drags two big suitcases, behind him. As the train pulls into the next station you can see your husband and two beautiful sons smiling as they await your arrival. You step off the train and into the arms of the people who truly love you and you are filled with a feeling of confidence and love. And that feeling will grow stronger day by day as you watch your boys growing up.'

I then finished the parts negotiation and the session.

Saying Goodbye

The Jacquin Girl-on-the-Train Metaphor - Script

Hypnotise the client and start whatever your preferred intervention is. At an appropriate time within your therapy session, start the metaphor.

'You are standing on an empty railway station platform, one of those old stations that you see out in the countryside. An old train pulls into the station, one of those trains with the slam doors. You open the train door and get into an empty carriage. As you sit down you notice that by your feet there are two big suitcases. The train pulls out of the station and moves down the track. As the train pulls into the next station you notice a man standing on the platform and as your carriage stops beside the man, you recognise the face, you know the smile. The man gets into your carriage and sits opposite you and when he speaks you know the voice. The train pulls out of the station and moves along the track.

The man's face, smile, and especially his voice spikes you with a pain from long ago, but not forgotten. I want you to be brave and do this and you will free yourself forever. Do this now: lean over to the man and thank him for any love that you shared, any pleasure that you had together and tell him that you forgive him.

Now, in those two suitcases is all the pain, sadness, hurt and any guilt that he left you with. Take hold of the cases and push them over to him and give them to him. As you do this the train pulls into the next station. Lean over and say goodbye, open the door and help him off the train with the suitcases and close the door. The train starts to move once again. You can still see his face clearly, but it starts to fade as the train picks up speed and the face just becomes a little dot in the distance and then disappears out of sight and out of mind, never to affect you again. As you settle back into your seat a feeling of peace and freedom sweeps over you. As the train pulls into the next station, you can see on the platform the people you love, people that love you. As you leave the train you can feel the love from the people there. From today the harder you and try and remember the hurt, pain and sadness the further away it goes. From today no matter how hard you try you will never experience it again.

One of the most famous lines from NLP is 'the map is not the territory'.

Meeting someone at their map of reality is something that we should try to do. If you can do this, you are more likely to build rapport with the person you are communicating with.

Below is a case in which I used this technique, but as you will see, rapport is not everything.

Out of My Depth

Very early on in my career as a Hypnotherapist, a young lady came to my office asking if I could help her brother who had been diagnosed as schizophrenic. She told me that although she and her brother were only in their twenties her mother was in her sixties and unwell. Her brother had not left his bed for days and her mother was desperate for help.

Although it was not my normal practise to do home visits, I agreed to go and see her brother at his mother's house. I went to the man's bedroom and when he saw me he was dismissive saying that I could not possibly help him.

He looked around the empty room and in a low, conspiratorial voice, said, 'There are people all around you that you cannot see. They speak to me all the time and tell me to do things—bad things. I have two people in my head that you cannot hear and no one understands what I am going through, no one believes me—they just think I am mad.'

Trying not to look as freaked out as I was actually feeling, I said, 'Dogs can hear things I cannot hear, birds can see things I cannot see. There are sound waves above and below my hearing range, but that doesn't mean they don't exist. Just because I can't hear or see anyone else in this room other than you doesn't mean that you can't.' He looked at me as if for the first time. I asked him what he wanted, and he explained that he wanted to be free of the voices and the fear.

I told him that I would use hypnosis and do my best to help him, and that all he had to do was allow himself to close his eyes and listen to my voice for a while. He agreed, and I proceeded to hypnotise him and give him suggestions for calmness and stillness of his mind.

I brought him out of hypnosis and as he opened his eyes he said that he felt much better and that the people in the room had left. I said that if he felt better, he should go down stairs and speak to his mother and sister, because they had been very worried about him, and to make them a cup of tea. He said he would and jumped out of bed and went downstairs. The look on his mother's face was priceless. I had been with him for less than thirty minutes.

Feeling very chuffed with myself and the miraculous change that I believed I had made in this man's life (this was in the days when I had an ego and was ignorant that as the therapist I actually did nothing other than facilitate the client's own ability to change), I left the house.

Two weeks later the man arrived with his sister at my office. At that time, I would sit behind a desk with my client on the other side while we spoke, and then I would lay them on a couch to do the hypnosis analysis (I knew no better at the time). The client's sister left and he sat opposite me on the other side of my desk. All of a sudden he stood up and started pacing the floor, nodding in agreement to some unknown and for-me-unheard voice.

He turned to me and said, 'Emily says not to trust you'. He proceeded to pace, nodding, and every now and then shaking his head in conversation with an unheard voice. Now this man was not a small fellow and I have to admit I started to feel very unsafe in my office with this man pacing up and down in conversation with the unseen Emily.

He turned to me with what can only be described as murder in his eyes and said in a voice that seemed to come from some dark place, 'Nobody knows what is going on in my head. I have John an axe murderer and Emily a kind, caring, women in my head.' He paused and turned his head to one side, nodding and agreeing with one of the voices.
He turned to me and said, 'Emily says to be kind.' I sat there thinking, 'thank f..k for that'. Then he turned to the other side and nodded and as he turned slowly back to face me, I swear his eyes had turned red (I have an imagination as well) and in a voice that seemed to be dredged up from hell and with spittle dripping from his mouth, he put his knuckles on the desk and leaned toward me, saying,

'Now do you understand what I am going through? Now do you see what is in my head? No one has heard my voice before.'

This I assumed was the voice of John, the mad axe murder. Glancing around my office quickly to see if by chance the cleaner may have left an axe out by mistake, I sat there silently, slowly getting showered with the man's spittle. Then just as suddenly as it had begun the client turned to the other ear and in a soft voice said, 'Emily says not to frighten you.' I sat there thinking, 'It's too late for that consideration.'

Trust me when I say it was as frightening as anything I had encountered in my life, but now that he was calm I said, 'I may not be able to help you, but as your sister is not picking you up for another thirty minutes, I will try.'

He agreed to lay on the couch and I proceeded to hypnotise him and do some work with him. His sister arrived at the agreed time to pick him up and he left. I went home to change my trousers. (only kidding).
I didn't see this client again, but some years later I was recalling the event to a friend (of course without using any names) and she said that she thought she knew who this person was and described him. I said I couldn't say, but I knew from the description that it was the same person. She said that he had recovered and that he had his own landscaping business now.

She knew his sister, who had told her that the whole sorry-scary business, had started one evening when her brother had been out drinking and smoking cannabis (marijuana). On his way home he had needed to relieve himself and in his drunken state had wandered into a church graveyard and urinated on a grave.

On realising what he had done and because of his drug induced, altered state, the thought had entered his head that he had become possessed. This thought grew and manifested in him the two imagined characters, John and Emily, whom he had introduced me to. I honestly doubt that his recovery had anything to do with the hypnosis—if it was I am pleased, but either way I am pleased he recovered, because I never want to meet John the mad axe murderer again, not even in my dreams.

As I have stated throughout this book, my belief is that any altered state offers an opportunity to give someone a suggestion or influence someone.

Love is one of the strongest emotions that we feel and is the emotion that I utilise the most within my work. Along with the power of imagination on our physical body. I demonstrate this to my pupils by asking them to imagine that I have a lemon in my hand. I instruct them to imagine that I have a knife in the other hand and to watch as I cut into the lemon. To imagine the juice running down my hand and to watch as I bite into the lemon. I then ask them ,what they are experiencing in their mouth. Most people will experience, their mouth watering, salivation, although I have no lemon in my hand. So we can't imagine something strongly without it having an effect on us physically.

Below is a case of mine in which I used the power of imagination and the wonderful emotion of love.

When it comes to physical healing of any kind, I make it clear that at this point in time 2018 there is no proof that hypnosis enables any healing to occur. I always make this clear to my client and say that ' I promise nothing' but I add 'what have we to lose, I'm not giving you any pills or potions. The worst thing that could happen is that nothing changes, so what have they got to lose?

A friend of mine who is a spiritual healer introduced me to a client of hers who had cancer, requesting that we work together with the lady. It was October and the client, a lady in her fifties, believed she was dying from the disease and feared that she would not live to see her daughter get married in the following January.

During the consultation I asked the lady a question, 'When did you decide to have cancer?' The lady looked at me with disgust and said, 'That is a ridiculous question, why would I decide to have cancer?' I asked, 'If there was a time, when would it have been?' The lady angrily said, 'I am not even going to answer. It is a stupid question.'

My friend did her healing and then I hypnotised the woman. I used the parts negotiation technique to help overcome the stress and anxiety that she was experiencing.

I then ran a guided imagery technique which involved using the love of her family to shrink and maybe destroy the cancerous tumour that was killing her.

I asked the lady to picture the people she loved, her daughter, son and husband. I asked her to feel the love that they felt for her like a burning hot sun in a summer sky.

I instructed her to shrink that burning hot sun down to a white hot ball of light as big as a golf ball, and to pull that ball of light into the very core of her being, to feel that light and love spreading into every cell, every molecule of her body, lighting her up and filling her up with that love.

I then asked her to imagine the cancerous tumour like a rock-hard ball of ice and to imagine that ball of ice melting away under the heat of that white-hot light. Then I gave her a post-hypnotic suggestion for self-hypnosis and encouraged her to use this ability to hypnotise herself and repeat the guided imagery on a regular basis.

I completed the parts negotiation technique and brought the lady out of trance. As she returned to normal awareness, she said, 'While I was in hypnosis I thought about that question that you asked me earlier—about when I decided to have cancer—which I have to say upset me at the time. Well, I lost my first husband to cancer when he was just forty years old.

'He and I were childhood sweethearts and we married in our early twenties, never having had any other partner or love other than each other. We had two children and a wonderful life together.

'When my husband died, I wanted to die myself. I couldn't imagine a life without him. Before he died—although he said he wouldn't accept it—I promised I would never love anyone else. I honestly believed I would not be able to love again. After my husband died, though, I did meet and fall in love and marry the man I am with now.'

I asked how that made her feel. She told me that although in her heart she knew that her first husband would have wanted her to be happy, she had an underlying feeling of guilt having promised him that she would never love again.

She went on to say that ever since watching the man she loved die so horrifically and in such pain from cancer, whenever she felt ill or in pain she wondered whether it may be cancer

I explained that the mind is super powerful and geared toward getting everything we are focused on and that it cannot process a negative. If all we are focused on is what we don't want, that tends to be what we get. Continually wondering and fearing getting cancer and having a feeling of guilt I believe is enough to bring it on.

The lady paid me and left. This appointment was on a Tuesday evening and I saw the lady again on the following Saturday. When she arrived, she told me that when she left on the previous Tuesday evening, she thought to herself, 'what a load of rubbish', but she said, 'I woke up on Wednesday morning and just knew that I would be alive to see my daughter get married, so my husband and I have bought our outfits for the wedding and booked a holiday for February.'

I told her how pleased I was for her and we did another session of hypnotherapy together. That was the last session of hypnotherapy we had together, and I didn't see her again until eighteen months later when I was driving through a little village in Kent. As I passed the village pond, I saw the lady walking her dog. I pulled over to say hello. She smiled and said, 'I know what you are thinking.'

I smiled and said, 'I am only thinking how pleased I am to see you looking so well.' She said, 'Since I last saw you my cancer has been in remission. I saw my girl marry, which if you remember I didn't think would happen and I have been relatively well since.' I wished her well and we said goodbye.

This was a lady who believed when I first saw her that she would not live for another two months and who was so ill she could hardly do anything. Was her recovery anything to do with the hypnotherapy and guided visualisation that I taught her—who will ever know?

It has been said that, 'Medication may not always be necessary but a belief in a recovery is'.

Physical Healing

I have never advertised and would never say that I am a healer. Many of my clients are suffering physically and some have cancer and other life threatening diseases.

As I said I never make any sort of claims or promises or charge any fee when it comes to healing. I simply ask the client who is suffering, 'What have you got to lose? I am not offering pills or potions—only words. The worst thing that could happen is that nothing changes, but what if?' To date not one of my clients has said 'no thanks'.

Below are the steps of this technique as I run it and my brief explanation of why it often works.

Quantum Healing

The theory behind this is that every cell in our body exists as an individual cell. All that makes you the unique individual that you are is a unique communication between those cells. There is, if you like, a blueprint in your brain of the perfectly healthy you. When we get a disease, there is a breakdown in the communication between those cells.

You now know and are proficient at setting up an unconscious communication. This technique utilises this communication, first using parts negotiation and then quantum healing.

Quantum Healing Technique

Hypnotise the subject.

'Now as you go even deeper into hypnosis you can use your unconscious mind as a resource you can learn from to gain unconscious strengths that you can utilise, to deal more effectively with those things, that had been a problem for you before, and all that is needed to build a good rapport with the unconscious, is to have a line of communication. Sometimes the unconscious communicates with movement. It may be that the eyelids flicker or the head moves slightly to indicate yes. It may be that the left hand moves all by itself and starts to feel lighter and starts to lift or drift up. Or the right hand goes even higher.

Only the unconscious mind knows which it will use, because your unconscious mind knows more about you than anyone else. And so as you drift deeper, deeper down into hypnosis I would like your unconscious mind to search and find one thing, one thing that is of utmost importance to your life, happiness and well-being.

Get a clear unconscious signal.

Ask the unconscious mind to hand the signal to the part of the client that is responsible for physical well-being and the immune system.

Get a signal.

Ask that part to make whatever changes and adjustments needed for the client to return to full well-being and to allow the signal to occur.

Get a few signals.

Ask the part to make those changes at a molecular level that will allow the client to be well again and allow that signal to occur when it has done this.

Get a signal and thank that part for making the changes.

Now ask if the unconscious mind would be willing to allow you to speak directly with every cell of the client's body, and if it is willing, to allow the signal to occur.

Get a signal.

Ask the cells to reconnect the communication that will allow the client to return to full well-being and health, and to allow the signal to occur if it is willing.

Get a signal.

Ask the cells to continue the healing process until the client is well.

Thank the cells for communicating and making the changes.

End the session.

Expect the Unexpected

Group Quit-Smoking Nightmare

For many years I ran group quit-smoking seminars throughout the UK, often seeing groups of up to 200 smokers. Running these groups was very satisfying knowing that you would change not only the client in the room, but also the lives of the people they loved by enabling the smoker to quit and be healthier and wealthier. These group seminars were also a lucrative business, as each client paid £65.00.

I was in Cardiff with two hundred smokers, all hypnotised and listening to my suggestions, when one man slumped out of his chair and fell on the floor. He lay there motionless and my immediate thought was that he had died so I went to him to see. To my relief I could see that he was breathing. Thinking he may just be in a very deep hypnotic state I started to count him up out of trance as I would do normally.

There was no response. I started to panic. My voice grew louder, almost pleading with him to wake up. Because of the situation, I had forgotten all about the lapel microphone I had on. Other people started to come out of trance. I was now beating the man on the chest and pleading with him to open his eyes. He coughed and smiled at me dazed and I sat him back in his chair. By now everyone in the room was sitting up in their seat wide awake, out of hypnosis.

I went back to the front of the room and my first thought was to apologise and tell them all to collect their money on the way out, but the people in the room represented a large investment and were in financial terms worth £13,000 to me. So, believing I had nothing to lose, instead of apologising, I held my hands up as if encompassing the group, and said, 'OK everyone back in trance', and every person in the room went back into hypnosis. Truly one of the worst moments of my life, followed by one of the most amazing moments of my life.

I completed the session in which more than 80% of the smokers quit the habit. The man who had collapsed emailed me personally to thank me for helping him quit the habit.

Identity - The Final Frontier

One of the hardest things for us to do as human beings is to change our identity, our persona, especially if we believe that it has value to us. I have often said that I would rather see a client for help with heroin addiction than someone for cigar smoking. Often clients come in with a self-proclaimed label: 'I am a junky', 'I am a smoker', 'I am an anxious person', etc. People will quite literally die for their persona. Below is a case in point.

A 43-year-old client came to see me for help with losing weight. He weighed 23 stone (322lbs/146kg).

He was a biker who rode a big Harley-Davidson motorcycle. He had shoulder-length hair which was going grey. He was wearing a sweat top, red tracksuit bottoms and calf-high black leather motorcycle boots. He reminded me of a middle-aged Father Christmas.

He told me how his father had died at 45 years old from a heart attack. My client's doctors had told him that if he did not lose weight, the same fate may be awaiting him. I asked him if he knew what weight he wanted to be. He told me that his doctor had told him that because of his diabetes and heart condition he should ideally be fourteen stone (196lbs/89kg), nine stone (126lbs/57kg) lighter than his current weight.

He seemed to want to live and I explained how hypnosis could help him, but he really had to want to lose the weight. Many different forms of therapy put a lot of value on what is known as secondary gain, the underlying value in the person's behaviour. Some therapists assume that there has to be another reason for people being seriously overweight other than the fact that they like to eat and drink. I personally do not assume anything. In fact I enter every therapy session believing I know nothing about the client's problem or the reason for their behaviour.
I asked Big John the Biker, 'Is there any good reason for being overweight?' He immediately and without hesitation looked me in the eye and said, 'No one gets in my way.' Now as much as wanted to help Big John, he and I knew in that moment that he would rather die than lose the weight.
At 23 stone, he was Big John on a big Harley-Davidson motorcycle. At 14 stone he was just an ageing biker, with grey hair, riding a motorcycle. There was no way Big John could live like that. He left, and I never saw him again.

The following story of a young heroin-addict woman makes the same point in a different way. The 32-year-old client introduced herself to me, in this manner: 'Hi I'm Mary I am a junkie'. I said, 'Hi, Mary. Now you have met me and you are no longer Mary-the-Junkie. You are Mary, someone who used to use heroin.'

The hardest thing for anyone, whether it is drugs or any other problem they want to overcome, is that to do so they have to change their accepted persona (who they believe they are). Very often they may also have to change their circle of friends.

It is very difficult even for the most dedicated and disciplined person to stay away from their chosen addiction if they are still moving in the circles that do it.

We all need friends and social contacts and changing your lifestyle completely and leaving your friends behind is very hard to do, but it is absolutely necessary if the changes are to last.

Mary's Story

Mary came to me out of desperation. She had been using heroin for fourteen years—since she was eighteen years old. She did everything to enable her to use the drug, sold everything—including her own body—to buy heroin.

She had, like most people, started with soft drugs. In her case she had been offered heroin by her boyfriend and thought she would try it. Mary was from a wealthy middle-class family, who lived in a wealthy middle-class town. She had been to the best schools and had had a good education, and underneath the wrecked body was a good person.

The saying 'there but for the grace of God go I', often comes to mind in my job. One step on another path—a meeting with one person—can change the direction of anyone's life.

I am amazed and feel it is a privilege when a client I have only just met trusts me enough to tell me their story. I saw Mary for a second appointment a week after our first hypnotherapy session and she had not had any heroin.

She then told me what she believed had set her on the road to addiction. Mary was just eighteen years old when it occurred. As I have often thought since being told this story, I think if I had been made to do what this girl had been coerced to do, I would have probably been on heroin.

The guilt that Mary had carried for fourteen years was immense. I used a psychological technique known as Time Line to help her.

The technique involves being hypnotised and going back to the initial event that caused the problem. This—as you can imagine—she was reluctant to do. (At the time when Mary came to see me I had not yet developed the 'Jacquin Time Machine Technique') I reassured her that if she was to do this she would be free to live her life once again without the need for any drugs.

We ran the technique and when she was back in her mind at the event, I asked her to look at it again with the understanding and the learning she had now at 32 years old, and to see who the guilty party was in that event, to notice that it was not the naive girl. I asked Mary to take the learning and the strength from that event and to let go of the emotion that was attached to it. To, in her heart, forgive herself, her father and her mother. I told her to give her younger self a hug and when she was ready to free herself forever to say goodbye. I used some very direct and some indirect suggestions and we finished the session. Mary completely overcame her addiction and when I bumped into her in town some years later, she had created her own business, and was enjoying her life, free of the need for any drugs.

The Power of the Spoken Word

As a hypnotherapist, language is a great tool available to me. If you are using hypnosis as a therapeutic tool or contemplating using hypnosis in any context, it is worth remembering the words of one of the greatest innovators and masters of hypnosis the world has ever known, the genius Milton H Erickson.

When asked if he was aware of the way he spoke, Erickson said,

'In any therapeutic work, you are going to use words to influence the psychological life of an individual today; you are going to use words to influence his life twenty years from today. So, you had better know what you are saying. You had better be willing to reflect on the words you use, to wonder what the meanings are, and to seek out and understand their many associations.'

In every hypnotherapy session I will use ideo-motor (unconscious) movements. The word is derived from the terms 'ideo' (idea or mental representation) and 'motor' (muscular action). As with reflexive responses to pain, the body reacts reflexively without the person consciously deciding to take action. This is supposedly direct communication with the unconscious mind. Whether it is a direct communication or not, I have used it enough times to establish that it is of immense use in human change work.

The idea is that you ask for an honest unconscious signal and wait for a signal to occur. This can be any movement: eye flicker, head nod, finger twitch, etc. Through this movement we can ask questions of the unconscious and change the underlying programming that is supporting the unwanted behaviour.

This next example is how this can occur in an unexpected way.

A client came for a second appointment, explaining that he really did not think he had been hypnotised at the first appointment. His reasoning was that he could hear everything I said. So, I said I would hypnotise him again and we began.

Sitting with his eyes closed and obviously thinking he was not hypnotised, I asked for a signal from his unconscious. With a derogatory smirk on his face he shook his head slightly as if to say, 'No way'. I of course said, 'that's right', at which point his head shook a bit more.

Now the look on the man's face changed from a derogatory smirk, in to a look of bewilderment, as he realised he was no longer shaking his head—it was just happening.

I continued asking questions and suggesting changes while at the same time asking for the signals to increase as a way of knowing that the unconscious was in agreement.

By the end of the session the man's head was shaking so violently, that it seemed that it may well fall off. The result was that the man had no doubt that hypnosis not only existed, but had nothing to do with relaxation, sleep or inability to hear. He quit the smoking habit and sent me many referrals.

For some years I coached boxing as an ABA coach. Although it was early in my career as a hypnotherapist, I had begun to understand the power of the spoken word and how belief in someone when communicated honestly can be a powerful agent for change. Below is an email communication from one of my boxing students which I believe demonstrates this.

Hi Freddy,

It's Sam from the Pembury Boxing Gym (TWABC). You were my boxing coach from around 1996 to 1998! I have been meaning to drop you a line for some time now. How are you keeping? It has been a long time!! I have always remembered the positive things you would say to me throughout my time training with you. You said that you were certain, that if you saw me in the street in 10 years-time, that I would be doing something with my life that I wanted to do and was worthwhile.

As I'm currently living overseas, and there's less chance of us bumping into each other in the street, I thought it best I email you! The things that I have done and I'm about to tell you about, I'm sure can be attributed to your kind and selfless support and investment in me at a critical time in my life, especially when I didn't have a dad around. So here we go...

You'll probably remember that I left TWABC to focus on my A level studies around 1998. I had never done particularly well at school, but surprised myself with 3 Bs, which at the time was fairly good! I chose to go to the University of Portsmouth to study Criminology and Criminal Justice. During that time, I briefly got back into boxing, had one bout against a boxer from Cambridge University, and won by 1st round stoppage. My strength had developed quite a bit from my time boxing in my mid-teens. I took my studies seriously and ended up with a 1st class Honours Degree (again I surprised myself, I was only expecting a 2:1 at best!).

Following this, in 2002, I decided to travel the world and do some work along the way. I spent a total of 2 years on the road and visited numerous countries across Asia, Central Asia, the Middle East, East Africa, and South America. I worked on and off during this time doing various voluntary jobs and also worked in a paid role a trekking guide, leading expeditions in Nepal, Pakistan, Morocco and Tanzania.

Not wanting to waste my 1st in my BA, I applied to do a Masters degree in Criminology at both Oxford and Cambridge Universities. Again, to my surprise, both accepted me. I chose to go to Cambridge and studied an MPhil in Criminology. During this time, I got back into boxing (remembering the ethic of hard work/training and the boxing skills that we honed in the gym over all those years). I had two competitions and won them both on points. The first was the 'town vs gown' bout, in which I won boxer of the night (from 22 boxers), the other was the 98th Oxford Cambridge Varsity Match (2005) in which I was taking on a 6 ft 3 (1.9m) southpaw who had recently won gold in the British Universities boxing competition. It was a close fight but I beat him and was awarded a 'blue', the very same sporting award that is given to Oxbridge rowers in the annual boat race. I never could have imagined that I would be doing this all those years ago training hard in the Pembury gym.

Just before I went to study at Cambridge, I became a Christian. This has been the most profound and life-changing experience of my 35 year life. My faith in Jesus/God (and a belief that God's heart bleeds for our hurting world) is the driving force for much of what I have been doing over the past decade or so. I became a humanitarian aid worker. Continued…

In 2005, I went to Pakistan to respond to the massive earthquake that killed 73,000 people and left millions homeless. I led a project in a tribally controlled area of Pakistan (close to the border with Afghanistan) providing shelter, medical assistance and livelihood support to people affected by the earthquake. I was there for almost 1.5 years. Following this I have worked all over the world: East and West Africa, Central America, Asia, and more recently in the Middle East. Over the past few years - since 2013 I have worked inside Syria - managing cross border aid operations from Southern Turkey, Yemen, and for the past 2 years have been working in the occupied Palestinian territory (Gaza, East Jerusalem and West Bank) as the Director of Programme Operations with the charity Save the Children International.

Oh, and I forgot to mention, I met my now-wife in 2009 whilst working in South Sudan. We have been married for almost 5 years now and are expecting our second child in just 3 weeks-time!

So anyway, this is just a little note to say thank you for investing in me, for your time and selfless devotion. It wasn't in vain and I know your efforts have contributed to me having the self-belief, hard work ethic, and determination to do what I have done, since I last saw you.

Thanks Freddy.

Following on from this story, let's think for a while about our own self-talk (the things we say to ourselves) and how these words influence our physical, emotional and psychological well-being now and in years to come.

I used to believe that hypnosis is a phenomenon that is created by a hypnotist or hypnotherapist to influence another person. Having hypnotised thousands of people and seen what hypnosis can apparently achieve, my beliefs have changed.

I still believe that what is considered to be a hypnotic state or trance exists, but I believe it to be a natural ability that you can learn to access at will rather than a strange phenomenon. This next section will teach you how.

Some people believe that hypnosis is like daydreaming or light sleep. Those states can be utilised to help you change, but they are not hypnosis.

Do you remember my definition of hypnosis that I gave at the beginning of this book? Create an emotion and give a suggestion.

The word 'suggestion' is often used by hypnotists and hypnotherapists, but what exactly does it mean? It's obviously a different meaning than a suggestion like 'Shall we have a cup of tea?'

A hypnotic suggestion implies that the hypnotised person will experience something, whether it be physical or psychological, as an act of non-volition, something that is happening to them as opposed to something they are consciously doing.

When you achieve self-hypnosis, you may experience a physical involuntary movement. This maybe a muscle twitch or a hand lifting by itself or any number of other movements. It may be that you apparently drift off into a sleep or experience a sense of relaxation.

There are only two rules when you are using self-hypnosis.

1) Always state the outcome that you want in positive language, e.g. 'I want to be fit and well', rather than 'I don't want to be ill'.

2) Give yourself time to come out of trance.

If you want to come out of hypnosis at any time just count to five.

The Jacquin Dream Architectural Therapy:

This is a guided visualisation technique to enable the client to search the depths of their mind for the answers and resolution of their problem.

Here are the bullet points on the next page is the complete script.

Induce hypnosis.

Guided fantasy.

Walk down five steps (deepener).

Garden fantasy.

Bench, sleep, into dream.

Field and valley fantasy.

River bank fantasy.

Rucksack, boat, unloading problems, limitations.

Visualisation, boat sinking to the bottom of the ocean, problems buried.

Laying back on the river bank and falling asleep.

Dreaming.

Centre of the mind, light, love.

Walking into the light.

Bank vault, combination, three numbers.

In the vault.

Safety deposit boxes, one with name on.

Photo, step in and experience having achieved their goal.

A folded paper, own handwriting, answer to problem.

Rewind.

D.A.T. Script:

You are standing at the top of a flight of steps, five safe steps that lead down into a beautiful garden. It is a safe secluded garden. You can see the flowers, smell the perfume, see the colours, hear the birds. As I count down from five and you walk down the steps, each step will take you even deeper into the most profound hypnotic state.

Five. Deeper and deeper.

Four. More and more relaxed.

Three. Free of all limitations.

Two. Even deeper.

One. A wonderful feeling.

Now you are in that garden. Feel the softness of the lawn beneath your feet, the fresh air in your lungs. You can see an old oak bench beside the lawn. You can smell the perfume of the flowers as you walk over and sit on the bench. As you look up into the blue sky you close your eyes and drift into a deep sleep.

As you go deeper, deeper asleep you start to dream. In that dream, you are walking through a field of gold: wheat, corn and barley, the kind of field that Sting sings about. As you walk through that field you can feel the softness of the plants under your fingertips. Watch the breeze moving the top of the plants like a wave on the ocean. See the golden hue as the sun glistens off those plants.

The field opens onto a wide, safe path that leads down into a valley. There are wild flowers as far as the eye can see, the colours fill your mind, and the perfume fills your senses. As you walk down the path each step takes you deeper and deeper into the most wonderful state. You can see ahead of you an old oak tree, hundreds of years old, its branches overhanging the pathway.

As you pass beneath the branches you can feel the coolness of the shade, see the light like diamonds shining between the leaves. You can wonder about all the people that have passed beneath these branches over the hundreds of years, people who have sheltered there, friends or lovers that have met there. As you walk back out into the sunshine you can feel the warmth of the sun on your face.

As you continue down the path, you can see the river that runs through the valley to somewhere miles away. You are now on the riverbank and as you watch the river flowing past, taking the leaves and twigs down the river, you can see an old rowing boat, the kind that you see in the park in the summer time. It is tied to the riverbank, left there forgotten about, abandoned.

You become aware of a rucksack on your back. You hadn't noticed it before, but now you can feel the weight of it. In the rucksack is every negative thought, limiting belief, angry word, sadness, irrational fear or pain that has been placed on you throughout your life.

As you feel the weight of the bag that has been slowing you down and holding you back, you can see me and feel me unstrapping the bag from your back. Watch, as I drag the bag over to the boat and heave it in. Watch as the boat goes lower in the water under the weight of the rucksack. See the boat drift down the river as I cut the rope and push the boat out into the current. See the boat get smaller and smaller and then disappear from sight.

Feel the feeling of freedom as you lay back on the riverbank and look up into the clear blue sky. Picture that tiny little boat way out on a vast ocean laden down with that rucksack. Watch as a wave washes over the boat and takes it to the bottom of the ocean, and with it every negative thought, limiting belief, all the hurt, pain, sadness and fear that had been holding you back and slowing you down. In your mind's eye picture that boat and bag being buried beneath the sand on the ocean bed.

As you do that, you drift off into a deep sleep. In that sleep you travel to the centre of your mind, the very core of your being. The space is filled with the most incredible beautiful light, like opening the curtains on a bright summer morning. The light floods your being with love and joy, filling you up, lifting you up. As you walk into the light you see a massive door in front of you, like a door to a bank vault. Three numbers pop into your mind and you punch them into the security keypad and the light turns green. You spin the dial on the door and pull the door open. Step into the vault, you can see a wall with safety deposit boxes on it. One of the boxes has your name on it.

Go over to the box and open the door, pull out the drawer and lift out the canister, take it to the table in the centre of the room. Lift the lid on the box and see a photo of yourself having achieved your goal. Step into the picture and feel what it feels like to have achieved it. See what you will see, feel what you will feel and hear what you will hear. Step back out of the picture and lift out the photo.

Underneath the photo is a sheet of paper, folded in half. Unfold the paper and notice written there in your own handwriting are the answers to the questions of what it is that you need to do to eliminate any problems and achieve the happiness and freedom you want in your life. You are memorising the answers and storing them in that part of your mind that is there for strength and learning to be used and utilised later on.

Once you have done that completely, put the paper back in the box, place the photo back on top of the paper and close the lid. Take the box back over to the wall and put it back in the drawer, push the drawer in and close the door. Walk back out of the vault and close the massive steel door behind you. Spin the dial and watch the light go red. The answers are now stored safely and securely in the centre of your mind.

Walk back into the light, think about the people you love, people that love you. From today every irrational fear and every ounce of anxiety will be gone and no matter how hard you try to remember how it felt to be afraid or anxious the further away the fear and anxiety will go. No matter how hard you try you will never experience the irrational fear again. As you continue into the light you realise you are in a dream that you are having while you are asleep on the riverbank.

As you begin to awaken on the riverbank you can remember the boat and the bag, now buried at the bottom of the ocean. As you walk back up the path that led you down into the valley, you can see the old oak tree whose branches you walked beneath. As you walk beneath the branches once again you can feel the coolness of the shade.

As you walk back into the sunshine you can feel the warmth of the sun on your back. You can see the field of gold and as you walk back into the field you can smell the perfume of the wheat and barley. As you walk through the field you realise you are actually in a dream that you are having while you are fast asleep on the bench in the beautiful garden. You are waking up in the garden and you can see the flowers, the lawn and the five steps that led down into the garden.

Walk over to the steps and as I count rapidly from 'one' to 'five' you are going to run up the steps with a new energy and an incredible lightness of being. 1 2 3 4 5. As you look back across the garden you can see the flowers, the grass and the old oak bench that you fell asleep on. As you look upon the scene you become aware that you are actually in a deep hypnotic trance listening to my voice.

It may be interesting to know that in that deep hypnotic state where thoughts drift by like dreams, some enter the mind and some drift through the mind while some are left behind to be used or utilised later on. Others are remembered or seem to be remembered at first, but then become more and more distant and forgotten over time. Time changes too, so you will know what a trip it's been when you begin to know that what seemed to be a short time was really a long time, or what seemed a long time was really no time at all.

And so, as I count from 'one' to 'ten' and you drift back up feeling absolutely wonderful, every suggestion given to you by me will be acted upon and become your reality. On 'eight' your eyes will open, you will feel incredible as if you have awoken from the most beautiful sleep. On 'ten' that feeling of freedom will continue to grow as you work toward your goals without thinking or trying.

Psychological Decapitation

This can be used to eliminate anxiety, negative thoughts or depression.

(Induce hypnosis however you prefer to do so.)

In a moment I will begin to count down from ten, and with each number down your body will relax completely, and that at the same time as I count down from ten, I will be counting up from one, and with each number up you mind will become stronger, clearer and more focused on what you want to achieve.

(Then start the count.)

10) Body relaxing, every nerve and muscle relaxing with every word I say.

1) The mind is stronger and more focused on what you want, how you want to feel and how you want to be.

9) Feel yourself relaxing more and more. Nothing bothers or affects you.

2) Every negative thought swept from your mind.

8) Body becoming completely anaesthetised, as if you have had a general anaesthesia.

3) Every limiting belief swept from your mind.

7) Dropping down toward a place of total peace, total relaxation as every word I say doubles that wonderful feeling.

4) The mind begins to separate from the body.

6) Going deeper, deeper down. Dropping down into a state of absolute peace. Imagine now that there is nothing you can do about it. The deeper you go, the better you feel.

5) The mind separates completely from the body and drifts away from the body. Drift out into the future and see yourself achieving the things you want to achieve and doing it fearlessly. Step into your body and feel what you feel having achieved your goal. Look back to now and notice all the things that you did to achieve that goal.

The mind drifts without boundaries and without borders.

5) The body drifts through time and space.

(Allow a few moments of silence so as to enable the client to experience weightlessness. Then continue with the count in this manner.)

Now as I continue to count down every number will double the feeling of relaxation.

4) Going deeper and deeper.

3) Dropping down further and further.

2) Deeper, deeper down.

1) Letting go of all physical awareness.

0) Now you are in that place of total relaxation and peace, where you have access to all you inner strength and abilities. Go even deeper.

Now as you go deeper, deeper down into hypnosis I will continue to count up from five.

6) Every negative thought that was ever placed on you is gone from your mind.

7) Every limiting belief that you or anyone else placed on you has gone from your mind. You cannot experience or feel them again. The harder you try to remember the negative limiting feelings the further away they go.

8) See the faces of the people you love, people that love you. Let that remind you of your real worth, your real value and just how loved you are.

Now feel that love like a burning-hot sun in the summer sky. Feel the heat and light from that love. Now shrink it down to a white-hot ball of light as big as a golf ball and pull it into the very core of your being. Feel the light of that love spreading into every cell of your body and flooding your mind with the most incredible feeling of empowerment and love. Feel the light of that love pushing that black cloud of doubt, anxiety and depression that has been on your chest up through your body. Into your throat, feel it moving under the force of the love and light. Feel it now just below your skull, and as I click my fingers it will be forced through the top of your head, never to affect you again. Get ready.

(Wait a moment and then click your fingers.)

Now watch that horrible black cloud drifting away from you. Higher and higher, further and further away. Watch as it drifts into space and gets sucked into a black hole, never to affect you again. And from today no matter how hard you try you will never be able to experience that awful feeling again. The harder you try to remember what it felt like, the further away it goes.

9) A moment of clarity where everything becomes clear, where almost anything becomes achievable.

10) A moment of enlightenment. A true understanding of your real worth, real value as a person as a human being and just how loved you are.

(Bring the client out of hypnosis)

Working with Children

I have often been asked whether it is safe to use hypnosis with children and my answer is an emphatic 'yes'. Why would you not use this natural psychological tool to help yours or someone else's child?

Earlier in this book we discussed metaphors and the power they have as an indirect way to convey a message to the unconscious mind that is less likely to be questioned and therefore more likely to be accepted and acted upon.

Once we understand the value of metaphor and storytelling and the way it can change the way we think and feel about life, we may begin to see how we have been exposed to this our entire life without really knowing.

A best-known book of powerful metaphors is the Bible. I realise that if you are very religious or someone who believes that the Bible is a precise historical account, then what I say next may offend you, but everything I write is just my opinion and only what I believe. As a book of wonderful stories with strong underlying messages, it is still one of the best there is.

Let us have a quick reminder of some of the stories of the Bible: Adam and Eve, Cain and Abel, The Tower of Babel, Sodom and Gomorrah, Moses, David and Goliath, Noah's Ark, Samson and Delilah, The Prodigal Son, The Farmer and the Seed, Daniel in the Lion's Den, Jacob and His Coat of Many Colours, and my favourite: The Good Samaritan.

Almost all the stories that we read or tell our children have a similar effect: Sleeping Beauty, The Ugly Duckling, Goldilocks and the Three Bears, Little Red Riding Hood.
We convey meaning to our children through analogies and stories. The way I work with children is by tapping into this natural—and for most children, incredible—ability to fantasise.

On the next page is how a general children's session will run.

I only ever see children with at least one parent present. Depending on the age of the child and their level of comprehension I will explain who I am and what I do and often describe it as a form of magic.

If the child is above the age of 12 years old I will treat them and speak to them as I would an adult, believing as I do, having had four boys, that the easiest way to lose a child's respect is to treat them as if they are stupid.

I will explain that we are going to tap into the power of their mind to help them overcome their fear or habit or whatever else they are there for.

I explain that it's all about the power of their imagination. I then demonstrate this by running the finger-lock induction on the child and the parent. Once their hands are stuck and they can't pull them apart, I get them to open their eyes and look at each other. This generally is a moment of laughter and fun for both the child and the adult. I ask the child who their hero is, depending on gender and age they will in general have some superhero or pop star. I make sure that the hero is a positive role model, not some dark evil character. I ask the child if they could imagine being that person, and so far every child has said that they could. If the hero is a film character the chances are that the child will have watched the film lots of times. If this is the case, then I explain that I will lift their left hand up and that as I do this I would like them to close their eyes and start to run the film in their mind. I tell them that when they see their hero in the film, to nod their head so that I know.

When I get the signal, I ask the child to step into the body of their hero and to feel what it feels like to be them. While they are experiencing this very altered state, I get very direct with my suggestions for the outcome they are there to achieve. I give post-hypnotic suggestions for confidence, fearlessness, etc.

I suggest that their right hand will begin to lift and as it does every fear will disappear, all their doubts about themselves will be gone. I continue with these kinds of suggestions as their hand lifts.

I will get them to open their eyes and watch their hands lifting. I give them the suggestion that whenever they want to use all their superpowers all they need do is say the name of their hero four times and they will immediately be able to use this power.

I ask them to close their eyes again and give a few more suggestions and ask them to run the film to the end and when they have done this their hands will drift down, and their eyes will open. I then wait for this to happen and end the session.

Because I have found that the majority of children find it difficult to concentrate for more than 30 minutes in a therapy-type situation, my work with children is normally carried out within that time scale.

I have found the use of anchoring to be a great therapeutic tool for children. They just seem to grasp the concept easily and enjoy the process.

Below is a description of how this is done.

1) In a moment, I will lift your left hand up to here and as I do that, close your eyes and start the film. (Lift the child's hand as you would in the Jacquin Power Lift Induction.)

2) When you see your favourite hero nod your head. (Get the signal.)

3) Step in your hero's body and feel what it fells like to be them. See what they would see, hear what they hear and feel what they feel. You are fearless, you are confident.

4) In a moment as you continue to be your hero in that film, your other arm will begin to lift all by itself. (Watch for the arm to start moving and continue to suggest that it feel lighter and continues to lift.)

5) From today the harder you try to remember how it felt to be afraid or anxious, the braver you will become and no matter how hard you try, you will never feel that fear again. The harder you try to remember the fear the braver you become.

6) You have a superpower within you. I would like that superpower to take your hands and pull them up and I want you to try and hold them still and find that they continue to lift.

7) Open your eyes and watch those hands lifting and from today whenever you want tap into all of your superpowers, you just repeat the name of your hero four times and you will instantly have access to these powers.

8) Close your eyes and step back into the film. (Give whatever suggestions and post-hypnotic suggestions you feel appropriate.)

9) In a moment your hands will drift down, the film will end and every fear you have had will be gone. The harder you try and remember that fear, the further away it will go. The harder you try the further away it goes. (Wait for the child's hands to drift down as you continue to give post-hypnotic suggestions. When the child's eyes open, immediately ask.)

10) Where has the fear, GONE NOW? Try and feel it and find you cannot. (Show the child how to tap into their superpowers (self-hypnosis) by repeating the name of their hero. Then finish the session.)

When you teach a child how to use their mind to overcome irrational fears and perceived limitations, you are opening up a world of possibilities before unseen and by default you are doing the same for the parent that is observing.

Jacquin Total Perception Management (JTPM) or (The Snap)

Total Perception Management

This is the ability to change any aspect of your life by changing your perception of who and what you are.

What if changing the way you feel emotionally was as easy as just changing your mind?

What if it has always been that easy and we just haven't realised it?

What if you were feeling anxious and you could just snap your fingers and no longer feel the anxiety?

What if the ability to change any emotional state could be achieved by just snapping your fingers?

Your brain is covered by a membrane and contained within an airtight chamber known as the skull. In a healthy person nothing gets past this membrane.

Your brain consists of nearly 100 billion electrically-excitable cells called neurons and many more neuroglia which protect and support the neuron. Each neuron processes and transmits information by electro-chemical signals. Each neuron may be connected to 10,000 other neurons. Every neuron maintains a voltage gradient across its membrane due to metabolically-driven differences in ions of sodium, potassium, chloride and calcium within the cell, each of which has a different charge. If the voltage changes significantly, an electrochemical pulse called an action potential (or nerve impulse) is generated.

This electrical activity can be measured and displayed as a wave form called brain wave or brain rhythm. This pulse travels rapidly along the neuron's axon, and is transferred across a gap known as a synapse to another neuron, which receives it through its feathery dendrites. A synapse is a complex membrane junction or gap known as the synaptic cleft, used to transmit signals between cells, and this transfer is therefore known as a synaptic connection. There is believed to be 100 to 1000 trillion synaptic connections within your brain. A typical neuron fires 5 to 50 times every second. The interactions of neurons is electro-chemical. Each axon terminal contains thousands of membrane-bound sacs called vesicles, which in turn contain thousands of neurotransmitter molecules each.

Neurotransmitters are chemical messengers which relay, amplify and modulate signals between neurons and other cells. The two most common neurotransmitters in the brain are the amino acids glutamate and GABA. Other important neurotransmitters include acetylcholine, dopamine, adrenaline, histamine, serotonin and melatonin.

This incredible complex process takes place within the closed airtight unit known as your skull. This incredible, complex process also describes a thought, a feeling, an emotion, a visual and audio representation and perception.

It's humbling to discover that all the things we believe to be real—including who we are, what we are, what we are feeling emotionally or physically, our moral or religious beliefs—are nothing more than the process described above and can be completely changed with a blunt instrument or a surgeon's scalpel.

Once you understand this and see emotion for what it actually is—just electro-chemically charged signals within your brain—you can decide whether you want to accept that emotional experience or not.

We have, contrary to the majority-held belief, more control over this complex process than we think. You can alter the electro-chemical transmitters with physical actions such as laughing, smiling and running, to name but a few that you can use to change your mind.

You cannot imagine something clearly without it affecting you physically and emotionally, even though it is 'just' your imagination.

If we are honest, we would accept that we often act according to the situation—sad at funerals, happy at weddings and births—even if we don't truly feel it at the time; to do otherwise would be deemed inappropriate. If you laugh at enough funerals or are angry or sad at enough weddings, laughing for no apparent reason, you may even be diagnosed as mentally ill. So in general we act appropriately—the emphases being on the word 'act'.

Integrated, perception, management (JTPM) enables you to change any emotion in the time it takes to snap your fingers. It enables you to feel no emotion, if that is your desire. It enables you to increase an emotional experience, if that is your desire.

JTPM enables you to completely reverse an emotion—sad to happy, angry to calm, hate to love—in the time it takes for your heart to pulse once.

Many of us indulge in our emotions, wallow in our unhappiness, bathe in our happiness, hold tight to our anger or perceived grievance and embrace our perceived self-worth, but none of this exists outside of the skull.

Shakespeare said, 'I could be bounded in a nutshell, and count myself a king of infinite space—were it not that I have bad dreams.' He obviously understood what I am suggesting here.

Imagine that you are experiencing a really bad day and feeling angry and frustrated and with the snap of your fingers—BOOM—no longer feeling that way. Imagine feelings of irrational jealously or fear, accepting that the emotion was irrational and deciding to eliminate those feelings and with a snap of your fingers—BOOM—you no longer feel it. Imagine that you are in a horrendous situation that you can do nothing about and the situation is affecting you emotionally and making you physically ill and with the snap of your fingers—BOOM—nothing connected to that situation has any emotional effect on you.

Imagine having the ability to experience zero emotion to any given situation or event. Would you be a lesser human being if you could switch off your emotions—or a more advanced human being?

JTPM will, if you decide to experience the process, empower you to take absolute control of your emotions.

The Protocol

Elicit from the client the emotional change that they want, both the positive emotions and the negative emotions that they want freedom from.

Give them the above outline of the brain functionality.

The client has to understand this concept and accept it. (If they can't, either because of cultural, religious or any other reason, it is probably not the technique for them.)

Once you have the agreement, hypnotise the client.

Run the Arrow Technique to eliminate the negative emotions.

Run the Arrow completely with the suggestion that when they drift back into their body with absolutely no emotion at all, that they go deeper into hypnosis and any remnant of emotion that they were aware of is now impossible to feel. Ask the client to nod their head so that you know that they are experiencing zero emotions.

Explain that you will snap your fingers twice and suggest that from this moment on whenever they want to feel zero emotion, that they snap their fingers twice and they will immediately feel nothing.

Bring the client out of hypnosis.

Examine the changes that have taken place. Test the effectiveness of the session by asking them to think of something that would have aroused a negative or destructive emotion and to experience the emotion. Tell the client to snap their fingers twice to eliminate that emotion completely. Confirm that this has happened. Test this a couple of times to be sure this has occurred. If for any reason they can still feel any emotion after snapping their fingers twice, rerun the protocol.

Continued...

Hypnotise the client again.

Run the Arrow again, this time placing the positive emotion in the target.

Run the Arrow completely with the suggestion that when they drift back into their body with the positive emotion, that they go deeper into hypnosis and increase the positive emotion. Explain that when the emotion is strong that they nod their head so that you know that they are experiencing it.

Explain that you will snap your fingers and suggest that from this moment on whenever they want to feel this emotion that they snap their fingers and they will immediately feel it. Examine the changes that have taken place.

Test the effectiveness of the session by asking them to think of something that would have aroused a negative or destructive emotion, to experience the emotion, snap their fingers once and immediately change that emotion completely to the positive emotion that they want. Confirm that this has happened. Test this a couple of times to be sure this has occurred. If for any reason they don't instantly experience the positive emotion after snapping their fingers once, rerun the protocol until they can.

Smoking Cessation

Although hypnosis as a therapeutic tool has a vast range of applications, the one that it is most associated with is helping people quit smoking.

There are more than 1.1 billion people on planet Earth that smoke. I know it is hard to grasp how many that is, so let me put the numbers in perspective. We speak of millions and billions, but here is the difference: a million seconds is 11 days, a billion seconds is 32 years.
1.3 billion people smoke cigarettes.

At the turn of this century the W.H.O (World Health Organisation) stated that in this century more than a billion people would die through diseases directly related to smoking tobacco. There is no other product or substance that, that claim could be made about, that would still be sold to our children.

Albert's Dream

Albert came to see me to quit smoking. e was 73 years old at the time and had been smoking cigarettes since he was thirteen. He had recently lost his wife to cancer and she had wanted him to quit.

I asked Albert if he wanted to quit and he assured me that he did. Then he told me something extraordinary. He said his one regret in life was that he had never owned a new car (I thought if that was his one regret, he must have had a great life), but he went onto say that he had calculated that he had spent the equivalent of £350,000 on cigarettes throughout his life.

Albert had never owned a new car. He walked out of my office and never had another cigarette, and he sent many people to me as clients.

I never found out whether he did achieve his dream, but I often think of Albert in some flash car driving through his town.

The Woman in the Yellow Rubber Gloves

A very elegant lady in her fifties came to see me to quit smoking. I asked her the normal questions, one of which was 'Why do you want to quit?'. She leant toward me as if there was someone listening, so I leant toward her.

In a very conspiratorial voice she said, 'No one knows that I smoke. When I smoke at home I put on a shower cap to cover my hair, I put on some yellow rubber washing up gloves and I go out into the garden. If it is raining I will also...' she looked around to make sure no one was listening and continued, 'get my umbrella and stand there in my shower cap and rubber gloves and have a cigarette.' She said that once she had had her cigarette she would go back into the house, take off her rubber gloves and shower cap, brush her teeth and spray herself with perfume.

She truly believed that no one in her family knew that she smoked.
At the very beginning of this book I explained my brief one-sentence description of how to hypnotise someone: 'Create an emotion and give a suggestion.'

Well, during the hypnosis with this client—and I don't know quite where the inspiration came or from where the touch of genius appeared—I heard myself saying the following words.

'You are in your next-door-neighbour's garden looking over the fence. The rain is falling lightly, and you can see yourself in your garden smoking a cigarette.

'You can see the yellow rubber gloves, the shower cap and you hunched under an umbrella and it starts to seem funny to you.'

The woman smiled. I continued.

'It seems ludicrous that such an elegant lady looks so ridiculous and it is getting funnier and funnier.'

The woman started to giggle and then laugh. I continued....

'It's hilariously funny and you will find it the funniest thing you have ever seen.'

The woman was now belly laughing. I continued.

'This is the funniest thing you have ever seen and you will laugh louder and more outrageously than you have ever done before.'

The woman is now almost falling out of the chair in fits of laughter and so I get very direct with my suggestions.

'From today the need for a cigarette will be gone. You no longer need or desire a cigarette. If anyone offers you a cigarette, no matter where you are, no matter what you are doing, you will smile and say "no thanks". From today the thought of smoking will seem ludicrous to you. You are a non-smoker.'

I continue to give these suggestions interspersed with winding the laughter up.

At the end of the session I gave the lady suggestions for amnesia for the session and she wondered why she had been crying. I told her she had been crying tears of joy. She agreed that she did feel fantastic, thanked me and never had another cigarette.
Sometimes laughter can be the best medicine.

I have personally helped more than 20,000 smokers quit the habit, and below is how I work with smokers. Whether individually or in groups of 200 people, the method and words are very much the same.

When working with a smoker there are generally three beliefs that are holding them to their habit.

1) I can't quit. (e.g. 'I've tried the patches, gums and the pills and I can't quit'.)
2) I am addicted to nicotine.
3) It is doing something for me.

I will explain how to destroy these beliefs and how important it is to do so, because if at the end of your session any of these beliefs are still in place, you will not be successful in helping that client quit the habit forever, with the emphasis on the word, 'FOREVER'.

Once the introductions are over and my client is sitting down, I ask the question, 'how can I help you?'. I ask this even if I know what they are there for, because I want a definitive, positive reason. If the client says, 'I need to quit smoking' or 'my wife wants me to quit' or 'my kids want me to quit' or 'I am dying and the doctor has told me I must quit', that is not, for me, a good enough reason.

I will ask the question again in this way: 'What do you want? Do you want to quit?' If, as they sometimes do, the client says, 'No, I don't want to quit, but so and so says I should for such and such a reason', I will tell the client that they have to truly want to quit and that it doesn't matter what anyone else wants. The desire to change has to come from within themselves or it won't be a lasting change.

I will sometimes suggest that they go away and over the next few days when they are smoking to ask themselves honestly, 'What am I getting from this habit?', and when they have made their mind up to quit forever, to come back and I will help free them from the habit forever.

Once we have an agreement that they are committed to quitting forever, I ask the following questions.

How old were you when you had your very first cigarette?

How many a day do you smoke?

What are you getting from the cigarettes?

Who are the most important people in your life? Who do you love the most?

Why do you want to quit?

How will you feel today, when you quit smoking forever?

Each of these questions has an underlying reason for asking them. I will explain by breaking them down.

'How old were you when you had your very first cigarette?'

The answer to this question gives me a few levers to use. Firstly I may use the experience of their first cigarette—which in general is not a pleasant experience—as an aversion during the session, and secondly if the client has a child or grandchild of a similar age, I will use that child as a comparison and the love they have for that child as an emotional lever.

'How many do you smoke each day?'

The answer to this question enables me to work out roughly how much in financial terms their habit is costing them over a year and ten years. They may be thinking in terms of £10 a day. I am going to project that to £40,000 over 10 years.

'What are you getting from your cigarettes?'

The number one reason I have found is the belief that it relaxes the client. Other top answers are 'I enjoy a cigarette', 'it's something to do when I am bored', 'it gives me a break from work', 'it's a reward' and very often the answer is 'it's doing nothing for me, it's just a habit I want to get rid of'.

It is important not to encourage or suggest their reasons for smoking—we want this list to be as small as possible. If the client says, 'it is doing nothing for me', your reply should be, 'So it does nothing for you, it is just a habit you want to get rid of, is it not?' This tag question 'is it not?' encourages the person it is asked of to reply in the affirmative.

Always ask this question, even if their answer to the above question is 'nothing': 'Do you enjoy any of the cigarettes you smoke?' This question is important, because many smokers will often say, 'I love my cigarettes', but when asked the question 'Do you enjoy any of them?', it encourages the client to think about it, and my experience has been that the answer is rarely more than four or five cigarettes.

You can break this down further by asking, 'Do you enjoy every puff of those four cigarettes?' The answer is of course 'no'. You can then say, 'So you may enjoy eight or ten puffs of smoke a day.' All of a sudden, the twenty or thirty cigarettes that they believed that they were enjoying has been reduced to eight or ten puffs of smoke a day. If you then compare that small amount of pleasure with one hour with their wife or child, you have very clearly put the enjoyment they get from their cigarettes into perspective.

I then say, 'So the big question is, are you ready to put that minute amount of pleasure, that you used to get from your cigarettes, out of your life forever?' You must get an agreement on this before you move on.

'Who are the most important people in your life, who do you love the most?'

I ask this because I will unashamedly use these people as emotional leverage throughout the session.

'Why do you want to quit?'

Now at this point we do the opposite of when we asked the question 'what are you getting from the cigarettes?' Where we wanted that list to be as small as possible, we want the list of answers to 'why do you want to quit?' to be as long as possible.

I will not wait for the client to answer, instead I start suggesting reasons in this manner.

'Is your top reason for quitting health?' I will get an affirmative, and then add, 'and your kids...', and looking up at the client say, 'because your children's lives absolutely depend on you quitting today. What about the feeling of freedom to be able to go anywhere, eat anywhere, fly anywhere without thinking "I've got to have a cigarette." That will be a great feeling, will it not?

(Let me quickly mention here because you will see this a lot throughout this section, the power of a tag question. A tag question are added to the end of a sentence to encourage an affirmative answer. Here are a few examples: Will you not? Can you not? Are you not? Could you not? Would you not?)

'What about the inconvenience, never having to stand outside in the rain, while everyone else is inside enjoying themselves, that will be great will it not?

'What about the smell, does that bother you? Never having to wonder if your breath or hair or clothes smell. It will be nice to know that your children and grandchildren will always remember you smelling clean, that will be good will it not?

'There's the money aspect. What you could do for your family with an extra £40,000 over the next ten years?

'There's your looks, your teeth, your hair, your skin—all of these are affected by your habit. I know it is surface, but you don't have to ask someone in their fifties if they smoke—you can see it on their face and skin.

'And there is the adverse image. It may have been a cool thing to do when you were young, but it's not anymore.'

The next question is a very early opportunity to give an embedded command, highlighted in bold.

'How will you feel when you leave here today and you "**quit smoking forever**"?'

Get an answer and make a note of it, because later on in the session you will use this answer a forward pace. If the answer was 'free', the forward pace may go something like this: 'See yourself out in the future, fit and well, watching your children growing up, and you living your life FREE of the smoking habit.'

Once you have asked these questions with your client, you set about destroying the three beliefs that we spoke of earlier.

The first belief of 'I can't quit' I destroy in the following way.

I now know who are the most important people in the client's life and I say this: 'If you had been to your doctor yesterday and he or she told you that if you were to have another cigarette you would die, the chances of you quitting are minimal.'

At this point the client will nod, because they have been told about all the health implications and still smoke.

Then I ask this question: 'But you have to ask yourself the question, if you went to the doctor and they said that if you have another cigarette that your child would die or your wife or your mother, you would quit would you not?'

The client has in my experience always answered, 'yes, I would quit'. I carry on: 'Have you got any doubt, if your child's life depended on you quitting forever, today, you would quit would you not?' When the client says 'I would quit', you have in that moment destroyed the belief that they could not quit.

The second belief—that they are addicted to nicotine—you undermine with facts that we know about addiction. Ask the client how long they have been smoking the same amount of cigarettes for. This will generally have been the same amount each day for many years. You explain that the definition of an addiction as described in all medical papers is that an addictive substance is something you have to have in your body to function and that to continue to get anything from that substance you have to increase the dosage or decrease the time between doses.

You point out to your client that they have been smoking the same amount of cigarettes every day for years, and that they haven't had to increase the dose or shorten the time between doses. You explain that at some point in their life they have settled on an amount of cigarettes to smoke each day based on one of criteria: finance or social acceptability—neither of which an addict has a choice over. I then make this statement: 'What you have is a habit, and that is why this has been so difficult to do.' I then ask this tag question: 'You can see a difference can you not?'

When they say that they can see the difference between what they have and what an addiction is, then you have undermined the second belief that was holding them to the habit. Because the major part of this quit smoking session will involve the parts negotiation protocol, explain how a habit is learned and turned into an automatic program, something akin to a part of you, and that they have a part of them that smokes.

The third and last belief that was holding them to the habit was that they believed it was doing something for them. The work you did earlier in breaking down the enjoyment factor has already gone a long way to undermining that value, but the other major perceived benefit is that smoking relaxes the smoker. Here is how I explain this belief away.

I ask if they have heard of Ivan Pavlov and his dogs. Many people have; some haven't. I explain that Pavlov was a psychologist at the beginning of the twentieth century. He had dogs in his laboratory and he discovered that because the people that were feeding these dogs wore white coats, that after a while whenever anyone in a white coat approached the dogs would begin to salivate in preparation to eat, even though there was no food there.

Pavlov named this physical response a conditioned response. It's a physical reaction to a conditioned stimulus. What Pavlov also realised was that Woof, Woof, we are animals too, and we can be conditioned.

When people first start smoking, and for the majority of the times after, they smoke when they are taking a break, they smoke when they are relaxing or having a drink or socialising. Because they smoke in these relaxed situations, as with Pavlov's dogs, we connect the two things in our mind: cigarettes and relaxation. Even though there is not one chemical in cigarette smoke that relaxes you. I then give my client this very direct suggestion: 'Now that I have explained this it will never affect you again.'

All the above is done before any formal hypnotic induction. I then proceed with the hypnosis, the parts negotiation (speak to the part that runs the smoking habit), direct and indirect suggestions, metaphors and post-hypnotic suggestions. As described in detail on the next few pages

Although this all seems a lot to take in and may seem that it would take forever to do, in reality a smoking session—whether it be one person or two hundred—will take no more than ninety minutes.

Quit Smoking Protocol:

Hypnotise the client with the Jacquin power lift + progressive induction.

Script:

Parts Negotiation:

As you go even deeper into trance, you can use your unconscious mind as a resource that you can learn from and really have an experience, one that is satisfactory to you. All that is needed to build a good rapport with the unconscious is to have a line of communication.

Sometimes the unconscious communicates by movement. It maybe the eye lids that flicker or the head that nods slightly to indicate 'Yes'. It may be the left hand that starts to lift to indicate 'Yes' or the right hand that lifts even higher. Only the unconscious know which it will use because the unconscious mind knows more about you than anyone else.

So as you drift even deeper I would like your unconscious mind to search and find one thing that is of vital and utmost importance to your life, your heart and lungs and your finances. When it has found it I would like it to allow me to know by allowing that honest unconscious signal to occur.

(*While the unconscious searches run metaphor*)
'As the unconscious mind searches the mind automatically moves toward those thoughts, idea and images that clarify most clearly for you the very things you say and do that seem to get in the way'.

Now I would like the unconscious to hand that signal to the part that runs the smoking habit and when it has taken control of the signal I would like it to allow me to know by allowing that signal to occur.
I would like to ask the part that runs the smoking habit to explain to (client's name) what it has been trying to achieve for them, what the positive function of the habit has been.

When (client's name) fully understands what the positive reason is I would like the signal to occur.

Now I would like the part that runs the smoking habit to go to the creative mind, the part that dreams, has ideas and creates plans and ask it to find lots of new choices. Other ways of achieving the positive intention of the smoking habit other than the way it has been doing. Something that has nothing to do with smoking, eating or any other chemical. Something that is of equal benefit or more that will allow them complete freedom from the smoking habit.

Each time it identifies a new choice, that it believes is at least if not more, immediate, effective and available, I would like it to allow the signal to occur. (Allow time for the search to occur)

Now I would like the part that runs the smoking habit to pick one of the new choices. The one that it believes is the most immediate, effective and available, and when it has done that allow the signal to occur.

Now I would like to ask the part that runs the smoking habit to take the new choice and integrate it into (client's name) body and mind and when it has done so, I would like it to allow the signal to occur.

I would like to thank the part that ran the smoking habit for communicating and allowing (client's name) the freedom from the smoking habit for ever.

(Time Machine smoking aversion)

That chair you are in is a time machine and as I click my fingers you will be sucked back through time as if time doesn't exist. Back to the very first cigarette you ever smoked, the very first mouthful of smoke that you ever tasted. You are going back with all the understanding you have now as an adult, as a parent. Drop down beside that younger you and put your arm around their shoulder as they take that first mouthful of cigarette smoke. You remember where you were and who you were with. You remember what that first mouthful of smoke tasted like, the disgusting taste, that burning sensation in the back of your throat, the dizziness and the nausea.

You can feel it now, taste it now. It's as if you have that first mouthful in your mouth now, you will feel sick but you will not be sick. As I click my fingers, that taste and feeling will get fifty times stronger. From today you will always connect two things in your mind cigarettes and the very first mouthful of smoke.

When you are ready to free yourself forever, give the younger you a hug, thank them for going through that horrible experience for you, tell them you survived it and say good bye step over the line into your future and close the door behind you, and leave the habit where it belongs in the past.

Suggested direct suggestions:
- From today the need and desire for a cigarette has gone from your mind and body.
- If anyone offers you a cigarette you will smile and say no thanks.
- I don't know whether it will be a minute from now and hour from now or twenty years from now when you suddenly realise you have been thinking about something else completely and the thought of a cigarette disappeared right here and right now.

Use your preferred Enduction.

Although this all seems a lot to take in and may seem that it would take forever to do, in reality a smoking session—whether it be one person or two hundred—will take no more than ninety minutes.

Good luck, change many lives.

Many 'drug problems' are actually problems of habit. These include (in my opinion) cigarettes (including cigars, pipes, e-cigarettes), cannabis, cocaine, and alcohol (with exceptions). Also, the recently added categories of gambling, sex, shopping, chocolate and even exercise. Depending on your opinion, if you are doing something consistently and it is of benefit, you are a highly motivated and disciplined person. If you are doing something consistently and it is detrimental to you, then you have an addictive personality. I read recently that Mount Everest is littered with the bodies of highly motivated, disciplined people. Habits can be good or bad depending on your perspective, but they can all be changed, ramped up or shut down with the use of hypnosis.

Weight Loss

Help with weight loss is something else that hypnosis is effective with.

I will describe how I work with weight loss clients and my thoughts on how and why it is such a major problem in the developed world.

Firstly, let me say that anyone can lose weight, providing they (1) truly want to lose weight, and (2) are willing to do whatever it takes to do so. Belief is a major factor when it comes to losing weight.

The majority of clients that come to see me for weight loss have already been on countless diets and weight-loss plans. Because of this, naturally their belief in their ability to achieve their physical goal is almost non-existent. As I have stated before, credibility is crucial if you are going to be successful as a therapist.

If you are overweight and are unhappy being so, you have (in my opinion) no right to sit in the therapist's chair and tell your weight-loss client that you can help them. If, on the other hand, you are overweight, but you are perfectly happy being so, then you have every right to say you can help your client.

I believe as therapists we don't have to be perfect (nobody is), but we should at the very least attempt to be the best we can be.

There are many reasons why people struggle to lose weight and it is imperative that we seek to determine what each individual's reasons are so that we can tailor their therapy accordingly. As with the smoking habit, there are a few commonly held beliefs that stop people from losing weight or gaining weight and then maintaining a healthy weight.

'I can't do it.'

If you remember from the chapter on quitting smoking this is a common belief that the majority of clients hold, no matter what the problem is.

'I am weak willed.'

'It is wrong to leave food on your plate.'

'All the women in our family are big boned.'

'It will be very hard to do.'

'I will have to go without all the foods that I love.'

There may be other limiting beliefs that your client holds that are stopping them from achieving their physical goal, and you will, through enquiry, establish what those are. This will enable you to undermine and eliminate those beliefs completely.

Remember beliefs are like soap bubbles and can be popped. So let us pop these beliefs. Here is how I set about doing so.

The first limiting belief: 'I can't do it.'

This is probably the easiest to pop. You will find countless situations in which the client would lose the weight. I could suggest a few, but that would be insulting your intelligence.

The second limiting belief: 'I am weak-willed.'

To pop this belief you will explain, as you have with other habitual behaviours, how we learn and how a habit—good or bad—is created. This leads into the discussion and description of parts which leads you to speak about the Parts Negotiation Technique. You could at this point use the finger lock as a demonstration of the power of imagination over physical control.

This conversation will give the client an insight and an understanding that although we think we are in control, the programming that they developed at some point in their life is running things automatically, out of their conscious control.

Limiting belief number three: 'It is wrong to leave food on your plate.'

I believe this to be a cultural belief, having been, as the majority of my weight-loss clients have, brought up in England. I know with certainty that the majority of my clients have been told that it is wrong to leave food on their plate.

There are a number of reasons parents give when instilling this belief in their child, but the number one reason is: 'there are children that are starving in the world and therefore you should not waste any food'. By this, what they actually mean is 'eat everything that is put in front of you, no matter how hungry you are'. This is, under normal circumstances (meaning without the use of hypnosis), one of the hardest habits to break.

Some years ago, whilst working with a large group of women who were seeking my help to lose weight, I said that I would suggest that as soon as their instinctive mind recognised that they had swallowed enough food to stay healthy and well, but at the same time lose the excess weight, that the moment that point was reached they would get up from the table and put whatever was left on their plate in the bin. A lady, with what only be described as a look of disgust on her face, said, 'I think that to waste food when there are starving children in the world is despicable. It's disgusting to throw good food away.'

The lady seemed to be at least four stone (56lbs/25kg) overweight. So I said to her, 'Take a photograph of yourself and send it to some starving child in Africa or India with a note saying "I have sent you this photograph so that you will know that I haven't wasted any food", and see how much better that child will feel. They will not feel one jot better. If you really want to help that starving child, start by putting food in the bin. After a while you will start to cook and serve yourself less food. If in doing so you save £20 or £30 on your shopping bill, send the child the money you saved.'

We sometimes say things just because we have always said them, without really listening to how stupid some of the things are.

> 'The willingness to accept responsibility for one's own life is the source from which self-respect springs.

Limiting belief number four: 'All the women in our family are big boned.'

This is my personal favourite and one of the most commonly used excuses/beliefs.

There are those reading this who I am sure have great medical knowledge and can undermine this belief.

My non-PC way of undermining this, and at the same time creating a positive emotion that I can then use to give a direct suggestion, is: 'I am sure that some people have bigger bones than others, but you will never see news coverage of thousands of starving children with one fat kid amongst them and people pointing at him and saying he's the big boned one.'

This usually will elicit laughter from my client, at which point I will give the suggestion 'the weight will drop off you'. Never waste an emotional spike to give a suggestion.

Limiting belief number five: 'It will be very hard to do.'

Many of your clients will have been trying to lose weight for years. Some will have lost weight and then put the weight back on and others will have been brought up in families in which the family members are seriously obese, and believe it is just a family trait. All of the above will have created negative beliefs within your client that losing weight will be hard to do.

Hopefully after a while you will have testimonials from clients of yours that have lost weight easily after working with you. Until that time, you must convince your clients that they must engage and invest time and energy into their quest to achieve their goal, but let them know that it will be easy and enjoyable.

Limiting belief number six: 'I will have to go without all the foods that I love.'

When your client arrives for their first appointment, the chances are that they think that you will hypnotise them and make them give up all the foods that they enjoy. This belief has been created and perpetuated through the idea of dieting.

One of the first things that I say to my weight loss clients is the following.

'I want you to forget about dieting. I give you permission to eat anything that you want, but this is what is going to happen. The need to overeat, comfort-eat or boredom-eat will be gone. You will eat what you want, but as soon as your instinctive, intuitive mind recognises that you have swallowed enough food to stay healthy, energised, satisfied and well, before the food even reaches your stomach, the desire to eat anything else off that plate will be gone.

'The physical ability to swallow any more food off that plate will be gone, and you will find yourself putting your knife and fork down. The feeling of empowerment that you will experience when this happens will be immense and the weight will drop off you. I want you to enjoy your life even more, enjoy your food even more. Over the next few months you will find a way of living that is fun and enjoyable. Enjoyable foods and fun ways of moving that will get your heart and lungs working and the weight will drop off you, easily, effortlessly and rapidly.'

So on to the actual therapy. A vast amount of the effective work is done by dispelling the limiting beliefs that hold the client to their eating disorder before any 'hypnosis' is done. Beliefs though are just one of the legs supporting the problem. Hypnosis and in particular the Parts Negotiation will help change the underlying program/habitual element of the problem.

Each client will present with their own version of the problem. For some it will be a case of portion control (the amount that they eat in one session). For many it will be a snacking problem (eating sweets, crisps and other fast convenient foods that are high in calories and low on nutritional value). For some it will a case of grazing (eating continuously throughout the day), and for some it will be a combination of all of the above.

I have found though that the common denominator in all of the cases of serious obesity is fizzy diet drinks, especially diet Coke and diet Pepsi. One of my goals during a weight-loss session is to get my client to completely give up these drinks. My advice—and that is all it is; it is not an instruction or a command—is that my client wherever possible avoids drinking calories. The client will then point out that on some of their diet drinks the words 'One Calorie' will be written.

I point out that if any of these major fizzy drinks manufacturers were to come up with a diet drink that worked, they would put themselves out of business within months. An ingredient in almost all fizzy pop is the chemical aspartame.

After we consume aspartame and it goes to the stomach, digestive enzymes break it down into phenylalanine (an amino acid), aspartic acid (an amino acid) and methanol (an alcohol molecule). Health effects from aspartame consumption are caused by these compounds which are absorbed into the blood.

I believe (my opinion once again) that these health effect of aspartame work against fat loss. As I stated it is in diet drinks and every client I have worked with on weight loss drinks these diet drinks. You of course can look into this and come to your own conclusion.

How you proceed with your weight-loss client will be determined by the above variations of the problem.

Below I will describe what has become known as the 'Hypno-gastric band therapy'. This involves the use of imagery while in hypnosis to run the client through a virtual gastric band operation. This convinces the mind that the stomach is very small, thus preventing the client from being able to eat more than a very small amount of food at any one time. This works really well for the client who believes they have to eat everything that is put on their plate.

This technique is really not necessary if the problem is snacking or grazing. For that kind of eating problem, suggestions for control and for elimination of the desire for sweets and snack food is a better option, I have found.

Let me state here that I believe that the majority of people are unfulfilled in some way. We are not always aware of this as a feeling of being unfulfilled, but more a feeling of need that there is something missing. One of our first instincts when we are born is to eat, so I believe that we often mistake this feeling of need as hunger and then we eat something. I believe this applies to anything that we find ourselves doing to excess. Rightly or wrongly, I proceed as if this is the case.

When running the parts negotiation I ask the part responsible for eating to identify what it is that the client needs to be fulfilled and to find ways of fulfilling that need that have nothing to do with food or any other chemical or drug, and to identify enjoyable healthy foods that will lead them effortlessly to their physical goal and enjoyable ways of moving that will help them achieve their goal.

Virtual/Hypno-Gastric Band.

Hypnotise your client and run the parts negotiation.

While the part is searching, run the client through the virtual operation.

This is my version;

You are on a hospital trolley, being wheeled into the operating theatre. You can see the surgeon and nurses and you can smell the anaesthesia.

You are being lifted on to the operating table.

As I count down from five your body will become completely anaesthetised. You will be able to see and hear but your body will be anaesthetised.

Five, every sensation leaving your body. Four, you cannot move, you cannot feel any sensations. Three, body completely anaesthetised. Two, every sensation gone. One, body completely numb.

You can see in front of you a TV screen, on the screen is a film of the inside of your body, you can see your stomach clearly on the screen.

You can see the look of concentration on the surgeons face as he prepares to fit the band around your stomach.

You see the surgical instrument with the band attached on the screen. Watch as the band is wound around the top of your stomach.

Watch as it is tightened around the top of your stomach, squeezing it to the size of a golf ball. Only 10% of your stomach is above the band.

The band is sealed in place and the operation is 100% successful. The screen flickers off.

From today you will be satisfied on a very small portion of food.

Below is a brief outline of my weight-loss session.

Ask pertinent questions.

Identify limiting and negative beliefs pertaining to the problem.

Set positive goal.

Discuss the formation of habitual behaviour, leading to explanation of parts negotiation.

Explain how you will proceed.

Hypnotise the client.

Run techniques: parts negotiation, virtual gastric-band (if appropriate).

End session and arrange a follow-up appointment.

(Picture of Jo Watkins who lost 5 stone and change her life)

The Dilemma

A lady came to see me for help in increasing her self-confidence. Her husband of 34 years had left her two years before and had recently taken up with a younger woman. The woman told me her sad story of how she had been married to her one and only love for 34 years. Together they had raised two beautiful daughters who were now in their late twenties. They had created a wonderful, prosperous business which had afforded them a wonderful lifestyle and life. They had all the trapping of wealth: beautiful cars, house by the sea and a yacht. Her husband had sold the business and retired, just before he had left her.

Although he had bought himself another house he still had a lot of his clothes and other things left at the family house. The lady had not insisted on him removing these things, because in her heart she hoped that he would return to her. But now that he was with another woman she felt that she needed the courage and the self-confidence to move on with her life, and that is why she had come to see me.

I listened to her story and then she said, 'You know my husband, he came to see you two years ago to stop smoking, which he did.' She continued, 'I'm not blaming you, but it was after he came to see you that he decided he didn't want to be with me anymore.'

Well as you can imagine, I sat there with my mouth slightly agape not knowing what to say. I have been accused of a lot of things, but splitting a marriage up by helping someone to stop smoking—well, that takes the biscuit. She told me that he was like a different man after he saw me: more confident and more vitality—some of which was probably because he could breathe properly for the first time in years.

I have stated a few times throughout this book that my goal in every therapy session is to give the person an understanding, an insight into their real worth and value—which goes beyond the stuff they own.

Sometimes with that new enlightenment comes an understanding of what they don't want anymore, things they may have just been putting up with or avoiding changing through fear or doubt.

When obstacles are removed, new possibilities often appear. I am not saying that is what happened in this lady's case; it is just a thought. Anyway, back to the story.

The lady told me that she was going on a cruise to Iceland in two weeks, and although she would still love her husband to come home and renew their life together, she may, if she felt confident enough, speak to other men on the holiday. I did the therapy session and bid her bon voyage.

Three days later a male client arrived at my office. As I do I asked how I could help. He said, 'You probably don't remember me, but I came to see you two years ago to quit smoking, which I did successfully—thank you.' He then went on to tell me that when he got home he felt really good, proud of the fact that he no longer needed a cigarette and felt full of life. He said he questioned himself as to what else he had been doing that no longer suited him or that he was unhappy with. Then he dropped the bomb, 'And so I left my wife.' Now I remembered him, of course—it was yacht man.

He said that he had recently met a much younger woman and they were dating, but the relationship had only made it clear to him that he was still in love with his wife. I asked him what he wanted and he said, 'I want to go back to my wife, but I have hurt her and my two girls so badly I couldn't ask her to take me back. I doubt she would want me back after everything I have put her through.' The man started to cry.

He continued, 'I have made such a grave mistake. She was and is still the love of my life and I have ruined it all.' My words to the man were exactly this 'Look, we are men, not gods, and we mess up at times. You need to forgive yourself and accept that we all at some point do things we regret.

Now I know it may not be correct procedure, but as he sobbed he could have been a 6-year-old boy. I went over to him and put my arm around him and for some unknown reason, kissed him on his bald patch.

Anyway, he didn't punch me which I suppose was a result. Now here is the dilemma: considering patient confidentiality and all the ethics about client privacy, what should I do?

Before reading on, ask yourself this question: 'Should I tell him that his wife had been to see me and had told me that all she really wanted was for him to come home, because she still loved him madly, or because of client confidentiality should I say nothing about her coming to see me?

Well, rightly or wrongly, I told him that his wife had been to see me. I told him that she still wanted him to come back to her and that she still loved him. I suggested that he waste no more time beating himself up and to go and tell his wife exactly how he feels. Fall on his sword, beg for her forgiveness or whatever it takes to let her know that he loves her, before she goes on the cruise holiday.

We said our goodbyes, and call me an old romantic, but I like to think of the two of them hand in hand on their yacht heading off into the sunset.

The Guilty Gangster

I was asked to travel to a country thousands of miles away from the UK to help a man with a sexual problem.

The man lived in a beautiful part of the world in a beautiful house with his beautiful wife. He claimed to love his wife and I had no reason not to believe him.

His problem was the opposite to the most common problem men present with, which is premature ejaculation. This client could not finish. He was capable of making love to his wife and they wanted a child together, but he just couldn't reach the point of ejaculation. No matter how hard he tried or how long he made love for, he just could not ejaculate.

I worked with him to resolve this problem over a number of days. On the second day, he revealed to me that he had a girlfriend who was pregnant by him. They had not planned for this to happen and he felt he had in some way been duped by this girl. He didn't love her, he didn't really care for her that much, but she was having his child. I know if you are a woman reading this that what I am going to say next will have you spitting at the page, but he said that he truly loved his wife and wanted to have a family with her, but he felt guilty about the affair he was having.

I can hear you shouting, 'rightly so'. His intention was to support his girlfriend through the pregnancy and to always support his child, but to end the relationship once the child was born. I suppose even if you are a defence lawyer and in your heart you know your client is guilty, it still remains your job to get him off the charge.

As a therapist and as a human being of course you will have an opinion, but I believe if someone is employing you to help them, then it is your duty (providing it doesn't go against your morals or beliefs), to do your best to help. My role as I saw it was to be able to help this man forgive himself.

.

Believe me when I say this was a very brutal man and I have no doubt there were a lot of things he had done that in the eyes of the law and mankind were far worse than having an affair, but all I wanted him to be able to do was forgive himself for the affair. This we did with the use of trance and general man-to-man, heart-to-heart conversations over the next few days.

He told me on day three of our work together that he had accomplished his therapeutic goal and he and his wife were overjoyed with the outcome.

Guilt is one of the most crippling of emotions that we can experience. In some religions guilt is the backbone of their doctrine.

We are sexual creatures and from very young age experience sexual feelings, although they may not be construed as such. To make a child feel bad or guilty for having these natural feelings is not only (in my opinion) unfair, destructive and psychological abuse, but also disgusting.

The next case also involves the feeling of guilt, but although again it is about someone with a sexual problem, it is the polar opposite to the one above.

The True Gentle Man

A young man came to see me because he was unable to get an erection. He was married, in love with his wife whom he adored and whom he found immensely attractive physically. They had been married for some years and a year earlier had had their first child.

Their sex life had always been healthy and they enjoyed each other greatly. For some months though the young husband had been unable to achieve an erection, making it impossible to completely enjoy each other as they had in the past. This problem was now affecting other aspects of his life. His self-esteem and confidence were low and this was starting to impact his job.

Having listened to his story, I asked if anything significant had happened to cause this. He said he had no idea why this problem had begun and reiterated that he loved and desired his wife very much. He had begun to think that it was physical, something he may have to live with and accept. His wife knew of someone that I had helped, and as is often the case, as a last resort they thought they would try some magic.

I hypnotised the man and using the Jacquin Time Machine I regressed him back to cause. I got him to re-evaluate the event, take the learnings and strengths from it, and let go of any negative emotions. When I brought him out of hypnosis, the look on his face was one of shock at the sudden realisation. I asked if he could tell me about the experience.

He said that during his wife's pregnancy they had not made love, because of his wife's belief that it may threaten the pregnancy in some way. They had waited until after the baby was born, by which time the young husband was naturally very keen on making love with his wife once again. Although his wife agreed to the lovemaking, in his enthusiasm he had inadvertently hurt her. This had made him feel so bad, so guilty for not waiting longer, that he had from that time on been unable to get an erection.

Knowing what had caused the problem and having revisited and re-evaluated the event—and most importantly, forgiven himself—the problem never occurred again.

By now you may have gathered that I believe hypnosis to be a natural state, albeit a very special one, and it can be induced by someone or entered into naturally.

I believe everyone should be able to use hypnosis and that it should be taught by teachers and parents to their children.

Below is a description of the techniques, some of which you have already learned in this book and some that you are about to learn.

This is the technique a I would use with younger children.

1) In a moment I will lift your left hand up to here. As I do that, close your eyes and start the film. (Lift the child's hand as you would in the Jacquin Power Lift Induction.)

2) When you see your favourite hero nod your head. (Get the signal.)

3) Step in your hero's body and feel what it feels like to be them. See what they would see, hear what they hear and feel what they feel. You are fearless, you are confident.

4) In a moment as you continue to be your hero in that film your other arm will begin to lift all by itself. (Watch for the arm to start moving and continue to suggest that it feel lighter and continues to lift.)

5) From today the harder you try to remember how it felt to be afraid or anxious the braver you will become and no matter how you try, you will never feel that fear again. The harder you try to remember the fear, the braver you become.

6) You have super power within you. I would like that superpower to take your hands and pull them up and I want you to try and hold them still and find that they continue to lift.

7) Open your eyes and watch those hands lifting and from today whenever you want tap into all of your superpowers, you just repeat the name of your hero four times and you will instantly have access to these powers.

8) Close your eyes and step back into the film. (Give whatever suggestion and post-hypnotic suggestions you feel appropriate.)

9) In a moment your hands will drift down, the film will end and every fear you have had will be gone. The harder you try and remember that fear the further away it will go. The harder you try, the further it goes. (Wait for the child's hands to drift down as you continue to give post-hypnotic suggestions. When the child's eyes open immediately ask.)

10) Where has the fear GONE NOW? Try and feel it and find you cannot. (Show the child how to tap into their super powers (self-hypnosis) by repeating the name of his hero. Then finish the session.)

Potensharu

In 2006 I developed a course for parents in which they would learn some of the techniques outlined in this book, along with some other powerful language patterns. I will describe the course and how the parents used the techniques to help their children.

As I have often stated throughout this book, all of the hypnotic techniques that I use can be found occurring naturally in everyday life, albeit at an unconscious level. When used specifically and consciously, they can be used to change behaviour and eliminate negative and destructive habitual programming.

Hypnosis can also be used to enhance learning, and on the course I described hypnosis as a heightened and natural learning state.

The course started with a description of what I believed hypnosis to be and what it was not (again just my opinion).

There are many negative connotations attached to the word hypnosis, and if these beliefs are not eliminated, people will not accept the use of hypnosis with children.

I explain that the reason hypnosis is so effective with children is because hypnosis utilises our ability to imagine, and children have a wonderful ability to use their imagination.

I demonstrate the power of the imagination by getting the group of parents to experience the finger-lock induction. The class was then asked to take a few minutes to answer honestly the questions below. This was to enable them to evaluate at the end of the course the changes within their child.

'Know Your Child, Know Yourself'

Please read through the list below and mark a score from 0-10 in the box to reflect your relationship currently with your child, 10 being several times a day, 0 being never.

Approval:

How often do you commend your child for the things they have done well? _____

Companionship and time together:

How often do you do things together and share experiences? _____

Conversation:

How often do you speak with your child about things of interest and importance? _____

Encouragement:

How often do you inspire your child through words and gestures? _____

Physical affection:

How often do you demonstrate love and care through physical touch? _____

Undivided attention:

How often do you focus on your child to the exclusion of anyone else or distractions? _____

Your Child

Please read through the list below and mark a score from 1-10 that you feel most closely applies to your child, 1 being the lowest and 10 the highest.

Honesty

Kindness

Confidence

Concentration

Sense of humour

Positive energy

Determination

Stress

Anxiety

Negative energy

Naturally Occurring Learning States

The Unconscious and the Conscious Mind

Our conscious mind is the bit of us that thinks it is us. It accounts for a minute amount of our total thinking capacity. The unconscious mind accounts for the rest.

Our unconscious, instinctive mind is very much the same as it has been for millions of years.

Although the area of the brain known as the amygdala is small (about the size of an almond in humans), it is the area of the brain that is the seat of emotions and helps run the fight or flight response. I like to think of the amygdala as the gatekeeper. Throughout our life when we experience pleasure or pain of any kind, in the moment of experiencing the emotion a picture or template is created within the amygdala. Once this template is created, for the rest of your life the brain will unceasingly scan the environment for anything that reminds it of the emotion, so as to protect you or lead you to pleasure.

From the moment we draw our first breath to the moment of our last breath, our unconscious mind is on. It is the unconscious that will smell smoke in your house when you are fast asleep or alert you to the creak on the stairs that shouldn't be there.

My theory is that your unconscious exists for two reasons: to protect you and to give you pleasure. It has been my experience that behind every behaviour your mind is only ever trying to achieve one of these things for you.

Your child's unconscious mind wants the same two things for them. And they are very simple goals: to be well, and to be happy.

Unfortunately, sometimes our conscious minds get in the way of this.

The analogy below was inspired by the book Training Trances written by John Overdurf.& Julie Silverthorn.

The Titanic Problem

A nice way to illustrate this relationship between the conscious and unconscious mind is to think of a captain and a ship. The Captain is the conscious mind, the ship is the body, and everybody else working on the ship is the unconscious. The Captain has an important job to do: to set the course or direction. The Captain checks that the ship is strong and sturdy. They also delegate: a good Captain expects the crew to do their jobs. The primary responsibility of the crew is to carry out the Captain's orders: in this sense, the crew is the 'doer', and it does everything else.

Unfortunately, many Captains have an inflated sense of self-importance: they have a particular chart of the world and that is reality as far as they are concerned. This can lead a Captain to stop trusting their crew to do their tasks or stop listening to them when they discover a problem that could potentially sink the ship. For example, the crew tells the bridge to slow the engines or they will break down, or the lookout shouts that there is an iceberg ahead.

Disaster can be averted as long as the Captain continues to listen to their crew. When the Captain refuses to listen, though, such as insisting 'it says on my chart to go 20 knots straight ahead', the ship is headed for disaster. Alternatively, the Captain may try to take over the crew's various roles as well, but when they do this they invariably take their eye off their key role and no longer set the direction properly.

However, if the second-in-command can convince the Captain to take a break and have an hour's sleep, the crew can slow down the engines, carry out the repairs and the navigator can steer the ship away from the iceberg.

When the Captain returns to the bridge, the ship is running smoothly and is back on course. Mutual respect and a clear understanding of their respective functions is the ideal. Smooth sailing is only ensured when the Captain trusts the crew to do their job and listens to the feedback they give and the crew calls on the Captain when something needs attention.

Your Child's Unconscious Mind

The unconscious knows everything your child needs to know about a problem or difficulty. It also knows everything they need to know to make rapid and lasting changes.

During the early years of development, a child also needs the guidance and protection of an adult.

Ultimately what the child believes will be shaped in their early years of life. This is a huge responsibility for the parent or teacher and should never be taken lightly.

'A belief is just a post-hypnotic suggestion given to us at some point in our life and what you are willing to die for will depend ultimately on what bed, in which continent or country and to which parents you are born.'
Freddy H Jacquin

Communication Between Our Conscious and Unconscious Mind

Most of the time the direct links between the conscious and the unconscious mind are closed on some level. Our unconscious minds keep us breathing, but—until we puff ourselves out—we don't give any thought to how we are breathing.

Sometimes, however, the links between our conscious and our unconscious minds are more open. Sometimes they are completely open. This happens most noticeably during the natural 'download' times that everyone goes into approximately every 90 minutes. We can think of this time as the time when our conscious mind passes all the information that it's accumulated to the unconscious.

At the end of the day the unconscious works out which bits of information to store where. It does this when we shut off the PC (our conscious mind) for the night and let the mainframe (our unconscious mind) carry out essential maintenance and upgrades, i.e. when we sleep.

Not sure that you ever have these download times?

Have you ever been driving and wondered how you managed to steer the last mile safely, because you have no recollection of it?

Have you ever been mid-conversation with someone and realised you've completely lost track of what they are saying?

Have you ever been doing a mundane chore such as the washing up and realised you were on complete auto-pilot for a while?

The chances are you've answered 'yes' to at least one of these. That experience was a download time, when the channels between your conscious and unconscious minds were completely open.

As the channels of communication are completely open during these times, any suggestion or experience given to us during these times will be taken on board not only by our conscious mind, but also by our unconscious mind. We therefore have access to 100% of our mental capacity during these times.

They are therefore a fantastic resource, so we like to think of them as naturally-occurring learning states

Children and Naturally-Occurring Learning States

Children go into naturally-occurring learning states all the time and at any time of the day. By watching your child you will learn when they are most likely to go into them. Common times are while watching the TV or a DVD, while playing a video game, while engrossed in play, in the middle of a tantrum, when they are upset, and in the time between consciousness and sleep.

The fantastic thing is that when they do, you have access not only to the 2-3% of their total mental capacity accounted for by their conscious mind, but also to the 97-98% accounted for by their unconscious mind. In other words, any suggestion given to them during a naturally-occurring learning state will be taken on board by 100% of their mental capacity.

This makes learning to recognise and utilise effectively your child's naturally-occurring learning states a hugely powerful tool.

Natural-occurring learning states are also useful because they suspend or bypass the conscious mind, where the main critical limiting faculty is held. It could be described as helping the child get out of their own way. They have tried to change a problem consciously and thought about it for a long time. It may have affected other areas of their life. Consciously they haven't found a solution. Unconsciously they know what to do.

Altered States

The barriers between our conscious and unconscious minds are also down when we are in an altered state, e.g. when we are moving from one emotional equilibrium to another or when we are experiencing extreme emotions. Children enter altered states more often than adults, for example when they get hurt or when they are having a tantrum.

We can trigger altered states in other people and, in particular, in our children. The easiest way to do this is to change their emotions. The most successful, positive way of doing this is to make them laugh.

Can you give your child a harmful suggestion?

The answer is yes you can and unfortunately probably have been without meaning to.

Remember, if you create an emotion within yourself or another person, then you can give a suggestion that will probably influence.

If you get angry and shout at your child and then tell them (suggest) that they are useless or bad, and this is done and said enough times, the child will begin to believe it to be true, and act accordingly.

'Your purpose in using Potensharu is to communicate ideas and understandings and to get your child to utilise the competencies that exist within them at a conscious, unconscious and physiological level.'

Positive Suggestions and Negative Commands

The most important understanding you can take from this course is the difference between a positive suggestion and a negative command. Both are equally effective in influencing your child's behaviour.

Providing you know the difference between the two and how and when to use them, you can greatly increase your ability to communicate with your child at an unconscious level and therefore avoid any resistance the child may have to your desired behaviour from them.

The Unconscious v. Conscious Mind

The unconscious mind is a super powerful tool and exists for two main reasons as we learned earlier: your protection and your pleasure—it wants you to be well and happy.

From the moment you take your first breath to the moment you take your last breath, your unconscious mind works tirelessly to achieve for you everything you desire.

The unconscious, instinctive mind is the same as it always has been since the beginning of human evolution millions of years ago. In contrast, the conscious, neo-cortex part of the human brain has only evolved over the last 200,000 years. This is the part of the brain with the capacity to reason and communicate through language.

Negatives – Do They Really Exist?

Negatives only exist in language. They do not exist in any other form in the universe. In the universe things exist; only in language do things not exist.

Only in language does it make sense to say, 'there isn't a black cat sitting by the door' if there is not a cat sitting there.

The unconscious mind is the same as it always has been, long before language and our neo-cortex were developed. Because negatives only exist in language, our unconscious minds cannot process a negative. To demonstrate this: DON'T think about a blue monkey. OK, what just happened?

The chances are you just pictured a blue monkey. You have to think of the blue monkey in order to tell yourself not to think of it.

This understanding works brilliantly in sales. Let's say you are selling a car and you know the criteria for your potential customer is that the car must be economical. If you say, 'This car is economical', they can choose to believe you or not; as adults, we can consciously choose to resist a command. But if you say, 'don't think about the 50 miles to the gallon you will get from the car, look at the quality of the paint work', the customer has to think of the miles per gallon. Their unconscious mind has no resistance to the negative command. The economy of the car becomes accepted, avoiding any conscious resistance the customer may have had.

Negative Wish Lists

How does this relate to your communication with your child? The easiest way to understand this is to start by looking at some sentences that are used by adults every day.

'I don't want to put on weight.'

'I don't want to be unhappy.'

'I don't want to be sad.'

As the unconscious cannot process negatives, it doesn't hear that part of the sentence. Instead, it processes the thoughts as:

'I don't want to put on weight.'

'I don't want to be unhappy.'

'I don't want to be sad.'

In other words, the only part it takes of the sentence is the positive.

'I want to put on weight.'

'I want to be unhappy.'

'I want to be sad.'

Because the unconscious strives to achieve for you everything you desire, but has no logic, and cannot process a negative, if all you are focused on is what you don't want, that is what you will get.

Negative Commands and Your Child

Exactly the same is true when we give negative commands to our children. Let's take a few sentences that most of us have used when speaking to our children.

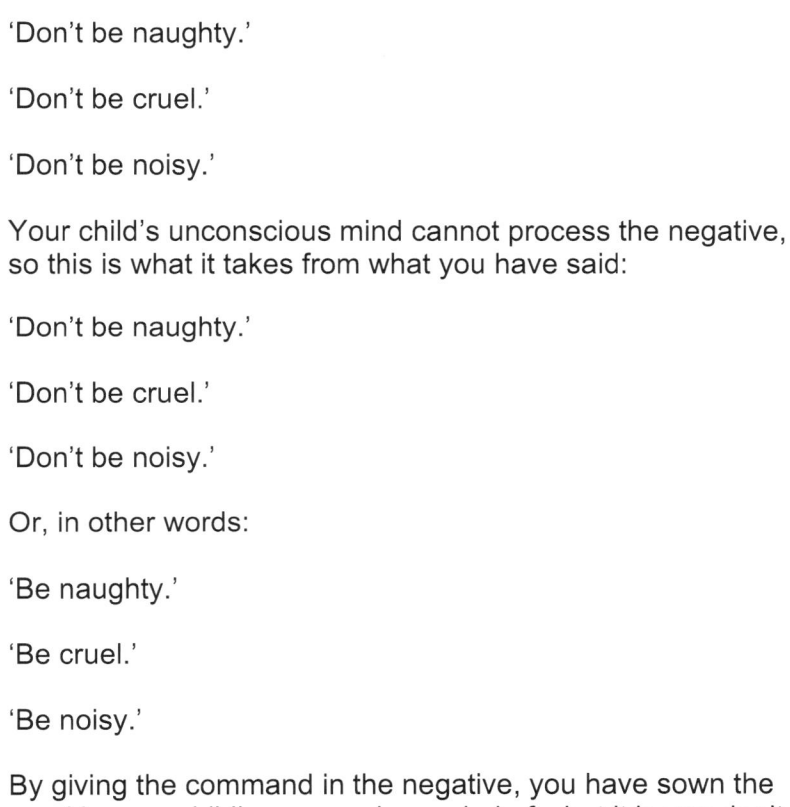

'Don't be naughty.'

'Don't be cruel.'

'Don't be noisy.'

Your child's unconscious mind cannot process the negative, so this is what it takes from what you have said:

'Don't be naughty.'

'Don't be cruel.'

'Don't be noisy.'

Or, in other words:

'Be naughty.'

'Be cruel.'

'Be noisy.'

By giving the command in the negative, you have sown the seed in your child's unconscious mind of what it is you don't want them to do. And very often that is what they will give you.

Positive Suggestions

The way to overcome this is to use positive suggestions. So, in the cases above:

'Don't be naughty' becomes 'Be good'.

'Don't be cruel' becomes 'Be kind'.

'Don't be noisy' becomes 'Be quiet'.

From today, whenever you hear yourself about to tell your child what you don't want them to do, immediately change your sentence to the positive. Don't just limit the power of positive suggestion to your child—whenever you hear yourself using the words 'I don't', adapt your thought to the positive, for example 'I want to be slim' or 'I want to be happy'.

Read this over until you have a clear understanding of the above, become aware of when you use negative language and wherever possible change your communication into a positive.

When to Use Negative Commands

Conversely, you can use negative commands to suggest what you want your child to do, while on the surface appearing to be commanding the opposite. Your secret weapon is that their unconscious has defence against a negative command. For example:

'Don't go to sleep.'

'Don't eat your vegetables.'

'Don't worry about kissing Granny goodbye.'

Try it – you've sown the seed of what it is you really want, and the results will surprise you!

First Technique: Anchoring

Overt Anchoring

Explain what you are going to do, e.g. place a resource or positive feeling into their hand.

Elicit the resource they need or want.

Explain the three things needed to achieve the feeling or resource:

Posture

Breathing

Internal dialogue

Set up physical anchor and trigger word.

Work with them to establish the feeling they want and anchor the feeling.

Repeat 3 times.

As they anchor the feeling for the third time use the direct suggestion below:

'From today whenever you need or want to feel the way you do right now, execute the anchor and hear the trigger word and you WILL immediately return to this feeling of confidence / calm / determination.'

Covert Placing of a Positive Feeling

Identify a positive resource or emotion that you believe would help your child, e.g. confidence, calm, joy, focus, determination, kindness, love, etc.

Notice when your child goes into the positive state naturally and anchor the state with a specific touch and a word.

REMEMBER, exactly the touch and the word.

When you want to elicit the positive resource within your child again, trigger the anchored state in exactly the same way with the same touch and word.

When this technique is carried out correctly, the child will immediately enter the positive state, enabling them to feel the positive emotion again.

To break through the fog, you need to become precise with your language. This will enable you to:

recognise the fluff when it appears

know how to ask questions to understand properly what it is your child really wants

get closer to your child's internal experience, enabling you to effect change more efficiently.

The technique below was first described in the book Unlimited Power by Anthony Robbins.

Using the technique, you will be able to become a precision language master, opening up effective communication between you and your child.

Technique to Precise Communication

The technique uses each finger of the right hand to represent a form of vague communication. The fingers on the left hand represent the counter-replies or specific questions you can use to blow away this fog to achieve effective communication between you and your child. Bring together the opposite fingers on your left and right hands as you think about this to reinforce what each digit represents and how you are going to apply this technique.

Right hand: 'Universals'

Left hand: 'All, Every, Never'

Universals are sweeping statements made to apply to everyone, for example 'everyone needs oxygen'. They are indicated by the words represented on the right hand: 'All, Every, Never'. When they are true, as in this case, they are fine: they simply convey a fact.

However, more often than not, universals are just a way of sending communication into the fluff zone. For example your child may say 'everyone is horrible to me', 'nobody likes me' or 'my teacher always tells me off'. In each of these cases—and for much of the time that we use universals—we have gone from a limited truth to a general untruth.

With the precision model, when you identify a universal, reflect it back to your child to encourage them to identify what they really mean.

Effective communication.

Blocks to communication.

Making an assumption is the mark of a poor communicator.

It is one of the most dangerous things we can do when dealing with our children.

Much of our language is wild generalisation and assumption.

Lazy language is the bane of all real communication. Lazy, over generalised language sabotages real communication

Communication Between You and Your Child

If your child uses vague phrases and generalisations when trying to tell you what is bothering them, you will be lost in a mental fog. The key to effective communication is to break through that fog by encouraging them to tell you specifically what it is that is bothering them and what they want instead. When you achieve this, you can deal with their problem and find a solution.

The most effective way of doing this is to repeat the statement back to them, emphasizing the universal quantifier.

For example:
Child: 'Everyone is horrible to me.'
You: 'Everyone is horrible to you?'
Child: 'Well I guess not, just some of the kids.'
You: 'Who specifically?'
Child: 'Nobody likes me.'
You: 'What, nobody likes you?'
Child: 'No, not everyone.'
You: 'Well, who specifically?'
Child: 'My teacher always tells me off.'
You: 'What, always?'
Child: 'Well, not always.'
You: 'When specifically?'

Statement: 'Should, Shouldn't, Can't'
Return Question: 'What would happen if you did? What causes/prevents...?'

If your child says 'I can't do this', what signal are they sending to their brain? A limiting one that makes sure that they can't do it. When you ask your child why they can't do something, they will find lots of reasons.

The way to break this cycle is to say, 'What would happen if you were able to do it?' Asking this creates a possibility that they were previously unaware of and gets them to consider the positive and negative by-products of the activity. You could also ask 'What prevents you from doing this now?', to help them become clear with what it is they need to change to accomplish the task.

Statement: 'Verbs'
Return Question: 'How specifically?'

Remember the brain needs clear signals to operate efficiently. Fluffy language and fluffy thoughts dull the brain. If your child says 'I am depressed or unhappy', they are not telling you anything specific, they are just describing a stuck state. They are not giving you any information that you can work with in a positive way. But you can break the stuck state by asking precise questions.

If your child tells you that they are depressed or unhappy, you need to ask 'How specifically are you depressed or unhappy?', or 'What specifically is causing you to feel this way?'

When you get your child to be more specific, you often must move from one part of the precision model to another. For example:

Child: 'I am depressed.'
You: 'What specifically is making you feel this way?'
Child: 'I'm depressed because I never get anything right.'
You: 'You never! get anything! right?'
Child: 'Well, no there are some things I do right.'

By breaking down the generalisations and being more specific, you are on your way to identifying a real problem and dealing with it. What usually has happened is that the child has messed up in some small way and made it symbolise some big failing that only exists in their mind. By communicating precisely you can help them narrow down what it is that is really troubling them and address that.

Statement: 'Nouns'
Return Question: 'Who or what specifically?'

Whenever you hear nouns—people, places, or things—in any generalised statement, respond with 'Who [or what] specifically?' This is precisely what you did with verbs—you go from an unspecified generalisation to the real world. You can't deal with a generalised limitation that only exists in your child's head. By challenging them to be precise you can identify the real-world problem that can be dealt with.

Unspecified nouns are the worst kind of verbal mist. How often have you heard your child say, 'they don't like me' or 'they're not giving me a fair chance'? Well, just who specifically are 'they'? If your child doesn't know who 'they' are, they can feel helpless and unable to change the situation, but if you can get them to focus on specifics they can regain control.

Statement: 'Too much, Too many'
Return question: 'Compared to what or who?'

Children often use this generalization, for example 'there is too much homework at our school' or 'there are too many things for me to remember'. When you reply with 'Compared to which other school?' or 'Compared to which other child?', your child then has to look at the reality of their statement and will most likely understand their true worth and potential and exactly what you are striving to achieve for them.

Once the child stops generalising and makes a judgement rationally using valid points of reference to make comparisons, they will naturally reassess their situation and move forward from a position of knowledge and strength. The phrase 'compared to what or who' will act miraculously on your child, opening up previously-unseen possibilities.

Additional Words to Listen Out For

Avoid words like 'good', 'bad', 'better', 'worse'—words that indicate some form of evaluation or judgement.

If your child uses any judgement words, for example 'that's a bad idea' or 'it's better to eat only vegetables', ask the question 'According to whom?' At the very least it will get your child to ask the question again and internally reassess the reasoning behind the statement.

Effective Learning

Working out your child's preferred method of thinking can help you to help them learn more effectively and help you to encourage them most effectively towards the behaviour and goals you think it would be helpful for them to achieve.

Representational Systems – Visual / Auditory / Kinaesthetic

NLP says that we all represent our experience internally through three main systems: pictures, sounds and feelings. What's more, people often have a preferred system. In other words, someone could be a predominantly visual person: when they think they tend to do so in pictures. It therefore makes sense to pace-and-lead to their preferred representational system.

There are two main ways to establish a preferred system. The first is to listen and the second is to look. Where one representational system is dominant there are likely to be physical and verbal clues.

Visual (Pictures)

Typically, people who are in a visual mode stand or sit with their heads and/or bodies erect, with their eyes up, and breathe from the top of their lungs. This is because they are thinking in pictures and have to try and keep up with the images in their head. This encourages them to speak quickly and therefore breathe in a shallow way at the top of the chest. They often sit forward in the chair or on the edge of the chair. They tend to be organized, neat, well-groomed, and orderly. They may be more appearance-oriented and sometimes quieter than others. They prefer to memorise by seeing pictures and are less distracted by noise.

Often a visual person will have trouble remembering verbal instructions and are bored by long verbal explanations because their minds tend to wander. They would rather read than be read to. A visual person will be interested in how someone looks at them, and will respond to being taken to places and being bought things.

Auditory (Sounds)

Someone who is auditory will often move their eyes sideways and also down to the right when accessing information. They breathe from the middle of the chest.

They typically talk to themselves and are easily distracted by noise. They often move their lips when they say words. They can repeat things back to you easily. They may find mathematics and writing more difficult and spoken language easier. They like music and learn by listening. They memorize by steps, procedures and sequence. An auditory person is often interested in being told how they're doing and responds to a certain set of words or tone of voice.

Kinaesthetic (Feelings)

A kinaesthetic person will typically breathe from the bottom of their lungs, so you'll see their stomach go in and out as they breathe. Their posture is often more slumped over, and they often move and talk sl-o-o-o-wly. Think of an actor who is playing a character who is absorbed in their feelings. They tend to slump physically, look down and breathe slowly. They will typically access their feelings and emotions to 'get a feel' for what they're doing. They respond to physical rewards and touching. They also stand close to people and touch them. They are often physically-oriented people (athletes). They may move a lot, and they memorize by doing or walking through something.

Predicates

Predicates are words and phrases which suggest the activity of seeing, hearing, feeling, etc. For example: 'I see what you mean', 'that doesn't add up', 'I need to get a handle on what you are saying'.

A person's use of predicates provides important information about how they are currently thinking and to which five senses they are giving greatest attention.

Predicates are a useful way of determining what system a person uses predominantly or with a particular experience. By noticing the words someone chooses when they are communicating, it's easy to decipher their preferred way of thinking (their modality).

Predicates can also be thought of as 'process words'. When a situation is perceived in an individual's mind, it's processed in whatever modality that person prefers. The words and phrases they use to describe a situation reflect that person's modality.

Once you identify a person's predicates, you can make it a point to match their language when you speak to them. Knowing a person's favourite thinking system enables you to literally 'speak their language'. This in turn enhances rapport and makes what you are saying more appealing to them and easier for them to understand.

For example, you present an idea to your boss, but your boss says they 'just can't SEE it working'.

If you modify your idea and then ask your boss, 'How do you FEEL about it now?' or 'Does that SOUND any better?', you have essentially performed the verbal equivalent of crossing your arms and turning your back on your boss.

Instead, feedback your modified suggestion in visual terms, for example 'Does it LOOK any better if I do this?' or 'Can you SEE the benefits more CLEARLY now?' By reflecting your boss's preferred modality, you will encourage them to reconsider your idea more positively.

Predicates and Representational Systems

Below are typical predicates a person may use, depending upon their preferred representational system.

Visual (Picturing Types)

Look at the bigger picture

It's black and white

It's all very hazy

Looks good

I have no focus

Get another perspective

Turn a blind eye

Brightened up my day

Auditory (Hearing Types)

We're on the same wavelength

Speak the same language

Music to my ears

Sounds good to me

It rings a bell

Tone it down

Kinaesthetic (Feeling types)

I feel great

Let's tackle this head on

I need to get a grip on things

He is as solid as a rock

She hurt my feelings

Need a helping hand

She rubs me up the wrong way

It all boils down to

Eye Movements - The Window to the Mind

We all move our eyes all the time. Yet, if you pay attention to WHERE someone looks, you can get an idea of HOW they are thinking.

Eye-accessing movements are the directions we habitually look when we 'go inside' to access and process information from our memory, imagination or feelings.

Where someone looks indicates whether they are imagining a future or past event, internally rehearsing a sound or making up a sound, talking to themselves or attending to their feelings. Being able to notice a person's eye-direction movements—and to recognise what they mean for that particular individual—provides information about how they are processing (or 'thinking' in the broadest sense of the term). Often, even the individual themself will not be aware of how they are thinking—yet the information is available if you know what to look for.

Let's say you are explaining to a colleague how to do something and they say they do not understand. If their eyes move up to either the left or the right as they say it, it indicates they may be visualising or trying to visualize what you are talking about. This could indicate they need you to demonstrate, rather than explain verbally, so they will be able to see how to do it.

Using Eye Movements to Encourage Learning

Although we all have our preferred modalities, ways of thinking, sometimes the way we think shows that we are accessing a part of our minds that may not be the most helpful reference point for what we are trying to achieve. For example, if your child has come to believe they are no good at spelling, when asked to spell a word, they may look down and to the right.

This means they are accessing the kinaesthetic area of their mind. In other words, rather than visualising how the word is spelt or hearing it spelt out in their head, they are checking out their feelings. And if they don't feel very confident about spelling, checking out their feelings is likely to make them feel less confident about the task in hand, so it's likely to become a self-fulfilling prophesy.

If your child is accessing the 'wrong' part of their mind for the task in hand, remind them literally to look inside themselves to see, hear or feel the answer.

For example, if they are struggling with a spelling, get them to look up and to the left to 'see' the word if they are struggling to play a piece of music they are learning. Get them to look towards their left ear to 'hear' how it should sound.

The Spelling Technique

Unfortunately, English spelling is pretty random, with very few hard and fast rules. Even the brightest of people can come undone with their spelling. But with the following technique, even people with dyslexia have become confident spellers.

Clearly write out the word your child wants to learn, broken down into syllables (remember that the conscious mind can only remember approximately seven things at any given time), for example:

Re-mem-ber

Albu-quer-que

Yest-er-day

Hold the paper with the word on it so it's at right angles to your child's left side, so they have to look up to see it.

Get them to read and spell out the first syllable, making sure they move their eyes up and to the left to read it, and don't move their whole head. Take the paper down. Repeat the technique twice more with the first syllable.

Repeat for each syllable.

Ask your child to spell the word back to you, getting them to look up and to the left to 'see' it.

For auditory types, saying the words of each syllable out loud, particularly in a rhythmic way, can be particularly helpful to reinforce this technique.

Metaphor

When we speak to others to communicate ideas, we often use metaphors, anecdotes and allusions. A metaphor is a story or tale that uses symbolism to convey a wider meaning or significance.

The Interpretation of Metaphor

When we hear a metaphor or see one conveyed in drama, it is not enough simply to listen or watch passively. To gain meaning we have to interpret it. We have to think about it, digest it, analyse it and relate it to our own understanding and experiences.

This makes metaphorical language work on a number of powerful levels.

The surface of the story is important, such as the strength of the narrative, the language used, and images created.

Metaphors stimulate creative thinking. The listener has to think consciously about the images and their resonances.

Metaphors provoke personal associations beyond the surface content of the story.

The meaning a listener derives from a metaphor will depend upon their experiences, understanding, intuition and beliefs.

Metaphors provoke an unconscious response. The suggestion of metaphor can bypass the conscious, critical reasoning and appeal directly to the unconscious, which will choose what is most helpful (as our unconscious wants us to be well and happy).

Metaphor in Hypnotherapy

As metaphor works on all these levels, prompting both conscious and unconscious associations, it is a hugely powerful tool.

Because the listener has to interpret the meaning of metaphor for themselves, they have to go inside themselves to use their own insight, intuition and creative abilities. Used correctly, metaphor can help the listener identify and deal with a problem on an unconscious level through the symbolism of the story.
By bypassing the conscious critical-reasoning faculty, metaphors can allow the unconscious to choose what is most helpful for whatever challenging situation the individual is experiencing.

Metaphors in hypnotherapy can be very generic or specifically targeted toward a particular outcome. They can last 20 minutes or 30 seconds.

Milton Erickson relied more and more on the use of metaphor throughout his work, because of the great value in utilizing the unconscious for both therapeutic and life learning. He also believed that the occurrence of amnesia following a story led to a better outcome due to distraction and non-interference of the conscious mind.

Advantages of Metaphors

Anecdotes are non-threatening.

Anecdotes are engaging.

Anecdotes foster independence: the individual needs to make sense out of the message, and then come to a self-initiated conclusion or a self-initiated action.

Anecdotes can be used to bypass natural resistance to change.

Anecdotes can be used to control the relationship.

Anecdotes model flexibility.

Anecdotes can create confusion and promote hypnotic responsiveness.

Anecdotes tag the memory—they make the presented idea more memorable.

The Power of Drawing Your Own Conclusions

None of us really like to be told what to do, right? If a pushy salesman tries to coerce you into buying something, you put up the barriers, don't you? As a parent, if you tell your kids to do something directly, more often than not you meet resistance. It's a natural response.

We all know that we can be far more successful in getting somebody to do something if we let them think it's their own idea.

Think back to the traditional story of the sun and the wind battling to prove who was more powerful. In the end, the sun won by persuading the traveller to take off the heavy cloak of his own accord by gently warming him. In contrast, when the wind attempted to whip the coat off him by force, that only made the traveller hold it closer.

Metaphor plays to this natural human response. The listener has to provide their own meaning to interpret the metaphor beyond its surface level. They have to draw their own conclusions, or—in the terms of hypnotherapy—have to provide a self-generated meaning. As they have to give some input themselves, they are likely to attach far more significance to the meaning they derive from the metaphor than if you had tried to tell them the same thing directly.

We can sum this up.

The therapeutic significance and impact of self-generated meanings are inherently greater than anything suggested directly.

Attaching Meaning to Metaphor

The best way to understand how self-generated meaning is gleaned is if we look at the stories and their characters as representing mental associations to possible mentors (role models, figures of power, guides) as facets of both the problem and solution. For example:

Parents could represent guides, sources of love and support, or sources of irrational guidance.

I can't do this, yet.
I am not good at spelling, yet.
I cannot overcome this, yet. I am not good enough, yet.
Suddenly, the thing you are talking about becomes achievable and achieving that goal simply becomes a matter of time and desire, how badly do you want this, how much time are you willing to give, how much effort are you willing to make?
Closing notes and suggestions to the course:
Lead by example:

Endeavour and strive to be the best you can be in your life, relationships and career so you to say to your child "You can achieve anything you want to achieve" and say it, hand on heart, in the knowledge that you are striving to be the best you can be.
Getting the most from this course:

Use the techniques, learning and understanding that you have gained from the Potensharu training to enable you and your child to discover the power of language, the power of the unconscious and the power and resources we all possess within us.
Strive to be happy and enjoy every moment with your child, take care of your body (it is the only one you will get), stay well and encourage and educate your child to do the same.

The Golden rule:
There is only one Potensharu rule, and that is that there are no rules.
Follow your instinct, you have within you, millions of years of evolutionary learning and development. Potensharu offers you some powerful psychological techniques, but you should only apply these through the filter that is your instinctive, intuitive mind.
If in doubt, trust your instincts.

A house built on contaminated land could represent a diseased body.

A colony of ants feeding on a particular tree in Africa could represent the immune system.

A child can represent the child within us—inexperienced and wanting to learn, but not knowing how; innocent yet spontaneous, with a limited repertoire of behaviours and responses.

Your Child and Metaphor

One of Milton Erickson's important principles is that people have in their own history the resources to overcome the challenges for which they seek help, even though they may not be aware of these resources. All you have to do is help your child find those resources to effect self-change. Metaphor can help you do this.

With quite ambiguous metaphor, suggestions and ideas provoke thinking that is applicable to anyone. Your child has complete freedom to discover a meaning. This discovery will be unconscious. A good metaphor will give your child enough to deal with to satisfy them consciously, too.

If your metaphor contains a child in it and you own child identifies with the child in the story, they are likely to feel hopeful as they learn how the child overcomes blockages to growth and freedom.

Building You Own Metaphors

Before you begin to panic about creating your own metaphors, take heart! As an adult and a parent you will already have developed a stock of metaphors that you use. Think of some of the stories you have told your child or to other adults at dinner parties.

Metaphors are a common part of our communication and we all have a stock of them ready to use. Some will be general purpose with universal appeal, some specific. It is not necessary to be a never-ending fountain of metaphors capable of generating a continuous tapestry of wisdom.

Many imagine Erickson to have worked this way—the truth is he had a stock like everyone else that he used over and over. Sometimes the 'same' story would take 10 minutes to tell, other times an hour.

To generate new metaphors on the fly, there are a number of things that can help you.

Use your child's metaphors. If in discussion your child uses an anecdote or symbolic language to describe themselves, feed it back to them. For example if they mention they feel like they are swimming against the tide, then use a metaphor to do with water and movement.

Use the problem to inspire metaphors. This means the metaphor has a slightly less ambiguous relationship to the problem and will contain inherent implications for fresh thinking and approaches to problem solving.

Draw inspiration from your own metaphorical associations. These can be simply based on the individual opposite you or experiences you have had or just whatever comes to mind. See where it goes!

Find a story, incident or slice of life that had an impact on you. Go over it once mentally. Let it settle in overnight. Recall it again and notice what the themes are and what other associations the themes stimulate in you. Let it settle in some more. Tell the story. Understand that the next time you tell it, it will be different.

Depending on your child and the outcome you want for them, your intuition will determine whether you think naturalistic metaphor (based on actual events or at least real things) should be used instead of fictional, allegorical stories. Preferably use naturalistic metaphor.

Metaphor is more conversational. To your child it may feel like you are rambling on about people you know or met

Don't spell it out for them!

Briefly divert attention after the metaphor. There is never any need to explain a metaphor to your child. Let them light up their own neural networks, make their own connections.

If you decipher it for them, you defeat the entire purpose of the technique.

Working with metaphor is a truly collaborative process that will keep your relationship with your children fresh and constantly evolving.

Self-Hypnosis

Whatever it is that you feel you need in the way of an inner resource—such as confidence, strength or determination—you can now build for yourself using self-hypnosis.

Whatever you need to eliminate or change within you—such as bad or negative habits, limiting beliefs, negative programming, emotional or physical pain—you can now change with self-hypnosis.

Ask yourself the question: 'How do I need to feel about myself? What belief would empower me to be able to be the very best I can for my child?'

Look within yourself: you will find you already have all the resources you need. What's more, you can now access them at will.

Rules for Self-Hypnosis

State whatever you want in the positive.

Give yourself a time limit. For example, 'I want to go into a deep, refreshing sleep and wake up at 6.30 am' or 'I want my unconscious mind to find lots of new resources for me. I've got 30 minutes.'

Trust your unconscious.

If you've got a question that you can't answer, trust your unconscious to come up with it for you. For example 'I've got 30 minutes. I want my unconscious mind to find the answer.' You may not get the answer you want, but if you can trust your unconscious mind and go with it, it can prove to be the right one.

'Our doubts are traitors, and make us lose the good we oft should win by fearing to attempt.'
William Shakespeare.

Objective:

Empowering your child.

A compelling reason to use all your resources is to do what you know you can do with your life to enable your child to achieve what they can in theirs.

We know that we have within us strengths, resources, and abilities that are rarely if ever used.

We have beliefs that empower us to achieve and encourage us to be good and kind.

We have beliefs that weaken our resolve to achieve, beliefs that may even lead us to be cruel or unkind.

Potensharu intends to enable you look at your beliefs objectively. In doing this we don't ask you to question whether your belief is true or false. Rather, we ask you to question whether a belief empowers you or weakens you, whether it motivates you towards being everything you want and can be, or whether it limits you.

Most if not all of our limitations are placed on us by others—some well-meaning, some not. What's more, you have absolute power about what you choose to believe.

The moment you recognise that most of the limiting beliefs you have about yourself have been placed on you, and that you have absolute choice in what you wish to believe about yourself, endless possibilities immediately appear.

Your Child's Beliefs

Your child already has a system of beliefs. These will affect what they think they can and can't do.

To find out what these beliefs are, ask your child what they believe they can or cannot do and seek out where those beliefs originated. You can then help your child to hang onto beliefs that empower them and put down beliefs that limit them by helping them understand that they can choose to hold on to only those beliefs that empower them.

Your Role in Shaping Your Child's Beliefs

Every day we are instilling beliefs in our children. We must understand that the words we use with our children and the meaning conveyed in our communication both verbally and non-verbally will not only affect their psychological and physical life today, but also their psychological and physical life thirty years from now.

We therefore constantly need to ask ourselves whether the belief we are about to instil in our child will ultimately empower or disempower them.

It is important to emphasise this awareness to you. As parents we must be willing to contemplate and reflect upon the words we use and the actions we take, to understand what their meanings are, and to seek out and understand how they will affect our children's life, happiness and development.

Goals

Defined goals are essential to help you achieve everything that you can be. Without a goal we are likely to lack direction and motivation. Goals give us a target. In setting that target we are already taking the first step towards achieving it.

The Potensharu Technique for Goal Setting

Many people set themselves goals—for example New Year's resolutions—without giving thought to what steps they need to take to achieve that goal.

By adopting the Potensharu technique for goal setting, you will not only set yourself goals to enhance your happiness and well-being, you will also empower yourself towards achieving that goal while making sure it is consistent with the philosophies and morals that guide your life.

This is important: if we set goals that are in conflict with our philosophies and morals—with what we hold to be important or dear to us—then our goals will create internal conflict within us that will ultimately undermine our desire to be the best we can for ourselves and our children.

The Potensharu Goal-Setting Technique in Practice

Establish the goal you would love to achieve.

Discover the beliefs that will empower you to achieve that goal.

Discover any negative beliefs that may prevent you from achieving your goal.

Eliminate negative belief.

I would love to ____

Empowering beliefs: ____

Limiting beliefs: ____

Suggested Technique: Positive embedded commands.

If the answer to question two is no, you need to re-think and re-establish your goals.

If in doubt, use happiness as your bottom line.

Suggested Technique: Future pace, plus ecology check.

Note: Your reason to take action toward achieving your goals will ultimately determine your ability to take action.

Accessing Your Child's Potential

PURPOSE = POTENTIAL = POTENSHARU

Your aim in following Potensharu is to enable yourself and your child to be the best possible, to overcome challenges and to access potential. There are steps you need to take to enable you to help your child achieve their full potential.

Self-Knowledge

The first step is to know what you need to do to enable your child to reach their potential. For example, you may need to be more available to help them with their homework; in order to do this, you may have to restructure your own week. Or you may need to give them more encouragement; in order to do this, you may need to become more positive yourself.

I need to: ___
To achieve this I would need to: ____

Motivation

The second step is to find a big enough reason, a purpose that will drive you to use all your inner strength and resources. It is one thing to be interested in helping your child achieve their potential. It is a totally different thing to be fully committed to enabling your child to achieve that goal.

If you say 'I would like my child to achieve their potential, for example I would like my child to go to university/be a musician/be excellent at sport', that's a goal, but it does not tell your brain very much. If you understand why you would like your child to reach that level of achievement—what it would mean to them, their quality of life, their happiness—you will be much more motivated to getting them there.

Reasons and Purpose

Suggested technique: Self-hypnosis to change negative internal representation to positive representation.

Accessing Your Inner Resources

Finally, it's worth realising that you're not in the starting part of your quest to be the best you can and to help your child achieve their potential from scratch. You already have a range of resources at your disposal that you can call upon to help you realise your goals. The trick is to access them so you can call upon them consciously and unconsciously as you work towards these goals.

Resources that can help you might include empowering beliefs, love, friends, skills, education, time, energy, financial resources, access to your unconscious resources and strengths, etc.
List all the resources you already have at your disposal to achieve your goals. Then take the time to use self-hypnosis to think about these recourses and to understand that by tapping into these recourses and strengths there is very little that you cannot achieve.

Resources
_____
_____

Suggested Technique: Self-hypnosis.

Assertiveness

Who's the Parent?

In any situation where decisions are made, there has to be someone who ultimately takes responsibility for that decision. When dealing with issues that affect our children—whether the issue is their safety, health, education or long-term happiness—someone must decide the best options. Potensharu wants you to understand that in these situations, if it is not you that is making the decision, then it is the child.

We want our children to grow up to be independent, social, confident adults and to learn to make decisions and judgements for themselves. As parents, we need to understand there are times when our children will want something or want to do something that we as adults recognise to be dangerous or just wrong for them.

We must be strong enough, assertive enough and believe in ourselves enough to make a decision and stand by that decision, no matter how much resistance we receive from the child.

As we have stated throughout the training, 'if in doubt, follow your instinct'—it will ultimately be the right thing to do.

This understanding—that as the adult in the relationship and as someone who loves them, you are in charge—must be established as early as possible in your child's life. It is very difficult when your child is a teenager (when they are surrounded by all the situations that teenagers face) to say, 'now you will do as I say', if you have let them have their own way as a child.

Self-Esteem: The Basis for Accessing Potential

Your child needs to have a true understanding of their worth—their value as a person as a human being—that goes beyond the way they look, the clothes they wear, the car they drive and the house they live in. Your child needs to respect their true self enough to be able to say NO to things that are offered to them that they know may destroy them. This belief and understanding of true worth and value can only be instilled within them by you, through your words of encouragement, your actions and your love. To this end you should establish this belief in your own true worth and value.

Suggested Technique: Self-hypnosis to establish self-esteem.

Small Words, Big Impact

Life changing words in the English language: realise, aware, because, yet.

Realise and Aware

Whenever the words 'realise' or 'aware' are used in a sentence, everything that comes after that word must be believed for the sentence to make sense.

For example, if you say to your child something such as 'eating your vegetables will make you strong', they can believe you or not.

If you say 'Tom realised/became aware that by eating his vegetables he became really strong', the emphasis of the statement is no longer on the connection between vegetable and strength: that is now a given. Rather, the action of the statement is Tom's new realisation or awareness, and the fact that vegetables make you strong is accepted without conscious resistance.

Because

If you say 'I want you to sit down and do your homework, it is important for your future exams', your child may not be aware of the reasoning within the statement 'it is important for your future exams'.

Now try adding the word 'because' into the statement: 'I want you to sit down and do your homework, because it is important for your future exams'. You then place an emphasis on the reasoning within the statement and your child will unconsciously accept and do what is being asked of them.

Yet

We tend to make statements as if they are done events:

I am not happy.

I am not good at maths.

I can't do this.

I am not good at spelling.

I cannot overcome this. I am not good enough.

If you hear yourself or your child using this kind of closed statement you only need to use one word to open up a world of possibility and that word is 'YET'.

Let's look at the statements above again and tag the word yet on the end and see what happens:

I am not happy, yet.

I am not good at maths, yet.

I can't do this, yet.

I am not good at spelling, yet.

I cannot overcome this, yet. I am not good enough, yet.

Suddenly, the thing you are talking about becomes achievable and achieving that goal simply becomes a matter of time and desire, how badly you want this, how much time are you are willing to give, how much effort you are willing to make.

Closing Notes and Suggestions to the Course.

Lead by Example

Endeavour and strive to be the best you can be in your life, relationships and career so you can say to your child, 'you can achieve anything you want to achieve' and say it, hand on heart, in the knowledge that you are striving to be the best you can be.

Getting the Most from This Course

Use the techniques, learning and understanding that you have gained from the Potensharu training to enable you and your child to discover the power of language, the power of the unconscious and the power and resources we all possess within us.

Strive to be happy and enjoy every moment with your child, take care of your body, stay well and encourage and educate your child to do the same.

The worst trait as a parent is needing to be liked by your child. Remember your are their parent not their pal.

The Golden Rule

There is only one Potensharu rule, and that is that there are no rules.

Follow your instinct. You have within you millions of years of evolutionary learning and development. Potensharu offers you some powerful psychological techniques, but you should only apply these through the filter that is your instinctive, intuitive mind.

If in doubt, trust your instincts.

Eliminating Negative Trances

How to Undo a Negative Trance Using Self-Hypnosis

Any behaviour—habitual or emotional—that appears to be happening automatically is trance.

Stage and street hypnotists often hypnotise people to forget their name or who they are. People can be made to feel incredibly sad or to laugh outrageously. They can enjoy eating an onion believing it to be a peach. They can be made to be petrified of a belt, believing it to be a snake.

Now as entertainment this may be fun for the audience, but in the mind of the hypnotised person on stage, these emotions and fears are absolutely real.

Here is the thing: in real life, believing something is a danger even though it is not or feeling sad or happy is no different from believing that a belt is a snake.

When we feel, love, hate, anger, jealousy or joy we accept these feeling as reality. 'I love her.' 'I hate him.' Then we act accordingly.

It may be a stretch to think of love or hate as a trance that can be ended in moments. I am not talking about the instinctive love we have for our children—I believe this to be hardwired—but the love we have for a sexual partner, in which the negative emotions of jealousy, rage, anger and the idea of ownership are often involved.

Let us for a moment discuss one of the most destructive emotions known to mankind: jealousy.

Although we are a highly-evolved species of animal, capable of sending machines to the outer limits of the solar system, we are still animals. We still have the basic instincts that we have had for hundreds and millions of years, one of which is to reproduce. We may believe we are in control of our lives, and one of our strongest instincts is to survive, but our genes are programmed for survival as well. The only way for our genes to survive is through reproduction.

Why am I talking about this? Well, we still function, when it comes to reproducing, at the instinctive level. We unconsciously search out partners that we feel have certain qualities that will give our genes the best chance of survival.

When animals mate in the wild, the male will separate the female from the rest of the herd for a period of time so as to give his seed the best chance to begin its growth within his chosen mate. The female will fight with any other female that has any interest in her chosen male for the same reason. Although we are no longer animals mating in the wild, the basic instincts still prevail.

Recognising basic emotions for what they are—outdated modes of instinctive behaviour—and an understanding that ownership can only be applied to objects, not people, is the beginning of our ability to overcome jealousy.

Fear is also a factor in the emotion, the trance, that we call jealousy. When we meet someone and fall in love, the feeling that you cannot survive without that person is often very strong. Of course, at some level we know we will survive the pain of separation, but we are programmed to avoid pain at almost any cost.

You may think that if we can switch on and off emotion at will that this makes us no more than robots. We don't have to switch an emotion off if we feel that it is providing us with something—pleasure or protection—but it is good to know that you have a choice.

Imagine feeling as if you have had your heart broken and then self-hypnotising and ten minutes later being free of the pain, or feeling depressed and self-hypnotising and deciding to be happy. How would your life be if any frustration you have could be eliminated in moments?

All of the above and any other destructive, painful or limiting emotion can be eliminated in moments by using self-hypnosis.

On the other hand, what if you wanted to feel immense joy or happiness, and you could create those feelings in moments?

Here is how we come out of a negative trance and leave ourselves in a positive trance.

Follow the steps for self-hypnosis as described above. Once you feel you are in hypnosis, you will give yourself a positive suggestion for how you want to feel. Visualise a future in which you are free of the negative emotion.

Then say, 'In a moment I will count to three and on "three", I will come out of the negative trance I have been experiencing, and be left in the positive trance I have put myself in.'

Count slowly to three. On 'three' you will come out of the negative trance, but your eyes will remain closed. Once again give yourself suggestions for your positive outcome.

Stay in trance until the allotted time that you have given yourself is up or count yourself out by counting from 1 to 5.

You can do this with any negative emotion or belief, no matter how long you may have had it.

Remember that trance is a natural state that we enter many times during the day. Emotion opens the portal to the unconscious mind and provides an opportunity to suggest something that will be acted on.

Prepare yourself with a handful of positive suggestions of behaviour or abilities that you want. When you notice that someone or some situation triggers a change in your emotional state, give yourself the suggestion or command that you want your mind to carry out. Never waste a trance state.